Nahima's Hands

Unique Mediterranean Cuisine

A Tantalizing Collection of Recipes
By
Andrea Cassell
and
Nahima Albert

Printed in the United States of America by Morris Printing Group

Copyright © 2010
Andrea Cassell

ISBN: 978-0-615-39933-1

Photography By:	Andrea Cassell
	Mary Sebastian
	Bruce Ward
Artwork/Collages By:	Andrea Cassell
Wine Pairings By:	Mike Murray
	Jamie Stratton

Thank you! Thank you!

<u>*Nahima Albert (grandmother)*</u>
You have been an amazing grandmother. As your first grandchild, you were an incredible role model. I look forward to the day we met again. Without your special love for cooking, there would not be a Nahima's Hands. Your hands are in my heart forever!

<u>*Della Zaher (mother)*</u>
You encouraged me with an abundance of love and patience. Without your tireless efforts, supplying me with photos, recipes and stories, there would not be much content. I am forever grateful for your tremendous love and support. I love you!

<u>*Joseph Zaher (father)*</u>
You gave me unconditional love and support through every step of this process. You are an amazing writer and I greatly appreciated your input. I love you!

<u>*Joseph Cassell (husband and lawyer)*</u>
You have always been my biggest fan and food critic. You have been supportive and patient during this whole process and allowed me to spread my wings. You are my rock! I love you always!

<u>*Debbie Brumbelow (my husband's legal assistant and now mine!)*</u>
What can I say...without your expertise and tremendous talents on the computer, I would have been working on this book for decades! You are a blessing. I have learned so much from you. You continually challenged me to seek perfection! I am forever grateful!

My precious children:

Bradley Steven Jr. (first great-grandchild)
You always eagerly wanted to learn about cooking from my grandmother, mother and me. You learned to perfect our dishes with enormous success. You have a gift for cooking! I love you forever!

Brent Steven (second great-grandchild)
What can I say...you can totally out cook me on some dishes. You created your own style and still kept the basic recipes. Your grape leaves rock! I love you forever!

Corey Steven (third great-grandchild)
You have learned the art of cooking by willingly assisting me in the kitchen. Without your love and support I could not pull off big events! Your tabbouleh is amazing! I love you forever!

Jordan Steven (fourth great-grandchild)
You are always there for me when I need a lending hand in the kitchen or on cookbook projects. You helped me with so many labor-intensive dishes. Your tabbouleh is fabulous! I am forever grateful for all your support. I love you forever!

Mark Lazzo (friend and lawyer)

You took time during your busy schedule to work on Nahima's Story. Thank you so much for your brilliant writing and editing skills. I toast you!

Karen Humphrey (friend extraordinaire)

I can unequivocally say you are one of the most amazing women I have ever met! I do not know where to begin to thank you for all the editing you did on the recipes. I know how much you have on your plate and you still found the time to help me. My life is so full of richness because of you and your special family. With love!

Laurette Lahey (friend, wine partner and engineer)

I had your unconditional support from day one! That means so much to me! You took the time during your busy schedule to edit my recipes. I treasure you and our friendship!

Wilma Jones (mother's friend)

I cannot thank you enough for collaborating with my mother and bringing Nahima's Story to life!

Teanne McKinney (dear friend and my agent)

For a year you stood by my side through many decisions and changes. You guided me with much patience and understanding as we went down this unfamiliar path together. I am blessed to have you as my confidant and friend. XOXO much love!

Mary Sebastian (friend, neighbor and photographer)

Thank you! Thank you for your willingness wanting to lend your photography talents to Nahima's Hands. You are an amazing photographer! So grateful for our friendship!

Bruce Ward (friend and photographer)

You have been there through all of my photo projects, always willing to collaborate with me on whatever I had, big or small. Thank you for sharing your talents with me!

Mike Murray (CS, CSW)
and Jamie Stratton (CS, CSW, CWE)

Thank you so much for lending your wine expertise to the cookbook. The wines you chose to pair with various recipes are perfect. Cheers to you both!

A special thanks:

Cindy Jacobs and Shari Hoffman,
of Morris Printing Group.

You allowed me to create my own style while being patient and understanding to the end.

Introduction

Everyone deals very differently with the passing of a loved one. A month after my grandmother, Nahima, passed away, I chose to put my heart and soul into this cookbook.

When I was 6 months old and the first grandchild, my mother went back to work as a first-grade teacher. She took me to my grandparents' house daily.

Antonio and Nahima owned a grocery store called Tony's Curb Market which was behind their house. Until I went to preschool at the age of 3, they would take me to work with them. I believe it was

there that I formed my personality. I learned the art of hospitality and personal relationships with vendors and customers.

I watched closely through the years as I got older, and witnessed my grandmother's passion for cooking. I can still recall the aromas from her kitchen as she tirelessly cooked amazing Syrian dishes for her family and friends. Even when she had a hard day at the grocery store, she still found the time to cook dinner for my mother when she came to pick me up from work. How could this selfless kind of love and compassion not affect me? Well, it truly did and created the individual I am today.

These recipes take on a whole new meaning to "comfort food." Cooking for someone else and using your hands in preparation is more than cooking; It captures the bond you have with family and friends. It brings us all together and enriches our relationships.

We all have our own connection with food. I use food through my traditions and entertaining, giving my guests the sense that they are part of my extended family.

In this day and age, cooking and entertaining in the home is a lost art that should be regained. You can't capture the true sense of sharing the love with others like you can in your kitchen! These memories will last forever!

I extend my hands out to you, as Nahima would, through the love of cooking. It will give me great joy and pleasure to have you prepare these delicious recipes.

May you share the love of cooking with your hands!

Enjoy! (Sahtein)

 Andrea

Nahima's Story – In Her Own Words

I was born Nahima Abouid on September 21, 1908 in Zedan, Syria. My father, George, died at age thirty-eight. I was three years old.

When I was seven, I remember being called home from school by my mother, Lula. My mother was near death. As I, my brother Naim, and my sister Cutlee stood at her bedside, mother kissed each of us on the forehead and told us goodbye. I remember mother looking at my aunts and grandparents standing next to us and asking them to take care of her children.

After my mother died, my siblings and I moved in with my aunts and grandparents. They were farmers and I became a farm girl.

I was fifteen years old when I met the man who would be my husband, Antonio "Tony" Albert. Tony had been living in the United States, working at the Ford Motor Company in Detroit.

Tony had come to Syria to see his relatives. Tony's family wanted Tony to marry my sister, Cutlee, and take her with him back to the United States. But Cutlee had another suitor, so I remember my relatives meeting with me and asking if I wanted to marry Tony. I said yes.

Tony and I were married in Syria on September 15, 1926. Tony spent all of his money buying dresses for my whole family for the wedding, as was the custom.

After we lived in Syria for four months, Tony sold a piece of property to help raise the money we needed to get to the United States. After living briefly in France and then Columbia, we had finally raised enough money to send Tony to the United States. Tony's best friend arranged for me to live with a Lebanese family in Cuba until I could get to the United States. Tony settled in Miami. He sent me $40.00 a month for my room and board.

When I arrived in Cuba, I was six months pregnant. My first child, Lee, was born there. When Lee was three, Tony sent for us and we left for Miami. My second child, Della, was born the next year in Miami.

Tony worked produce in a grocery store owned by his friend Habeshee. Tony worked a long time to get the money to build his own store. He called it "Tony's Curb Market". He built a large room at the back of the store for us to live. My third child, Mary Jane, was born there four years later. My youngest child, Sammy, was born four years after Mary Jane.

We were outgrowing our living space. When a man told Tony that he would sell him two lots behind the store on the next street, 80th Street, to build a house, Tony bought it and built our house there.

My husband Tony passed away September 24, 1984. I lived the rest of my life in the house that Tony and I built on 80th Street.

*Nahima Abouid passed away on August 2, 2009. She left four children, ten grandchildren, and twenty-one great grand-children.

Glossary of Terms and Ingredients
with Arabic pronunciation

*These items can be found at international food stores.

Spices and Herbs

Allspice (Bhar)   Tastes like a mixture of cloves, cinnamon and nutmeg. Good with vegetables and meat dishes.

Anise (Yansoon)   Ancient Egyptians and Romans cultivated it for its fragrance, flavor and medicinal properties. The seed is crushed and considered a spice. Used in many savory dishes and desserts.

Basil (Habak)   Was called the "royal herb" by ancient Greeks. Is a key herb in Mediterranean cooking. Used in salads, vegetables and soups.

Cinnamon (Kirfee)   An age old spice used by Egyptians and wealthy Romans. Has a mild sweet flavor. Used in savory meats, vegetables and desserts.

Coriander (Kizbara)   A native to the Mediterranean and is related to the parsley family. The leaves are commonly known as cilantro. Has a pungent flavor and odor. Use in highly seasoned food.

Cumin (Kamon)   *An ancient spice that dates back to the Old Testament. An aromatic nutty flavor with a slightly bitter taste. Used to season vegetables, stews and meatless dishes.*

Fennel Seed (Shomra) *Cultivated throughout the Mediterranean and the United States. Used whole or ground in savory dishes or sweets.*

Garlic (Thume)   *Throughout the centuries, garlic was thought to possess magical powers. Has many medicinal properties. Used all over the world in hundreds of dishes.*

Kisch*   *A powdered, dried yogurt used in soups. Created by Syrians.*

Mahleb*   *A small seed from the stone of a wild cherry. Used in dough and pastries.*

Marjoram (Mardokosh)   *The Greeks call it the joy of the mountain. Related to oregano with a slightly bitter taste. Used in salads, beef, veal, lamb, poultry, fish and vegetables.*

Mint (Na'na)   *A symbol of hospitality by the Greeks. A very aromatic herb with a cool and sweet flavor. Used in soups, salads and beverages.*

Nutmeg (Joze Alteeb) Native to the Spice Islands. The seed is from the nutmeg tree (a tropical evergreen). Flavor and aroma is spicy and sweet. Can be used in vegetables, meats, custards, desserts and seasonings.

Oregano Soldiers in World War II came back from Italy raving about this herb. Goes well with tomato-based dishes, soups and stews.

Paprika Hungarians have used this for many years. A powder substance made from grinding sweet red pepper pods. Paprika is now widely used in many countries. Can be used in many savory dishes or as a garnish.

Parsley (Bakdounes) In ancient times, parsley wreaths were used to ward off drunkenness. Has a very gentle flavor. Curly and flat-leaf varieties are used in cooking and garnishes. Goes well with all foods except sweets. An important staple in the Middle East in dishes such as tabbouleh salad.

Rosemary Has been around since 500 B.C. Is native to the Mediterranean area. Can be used in a variety of dishes such as meats, lamb, fish, eggs, stuffing, dressings, vegetables, soups and stews.

Saffron

One of the most expensive spices. It originates from a small purple crocus. Each flower has three stigmas which are hand-picked carefully and dried. It is very labor intensive. The threads need to be crushed before adding to a dish. Has a deep yellow color and is perfect to season rice, soups, stews and vegetable dishes.

Sage

Has been around for centuries in Mediterranean countries. It has a pungent, musty mint and slightly bitter taste and aroma. Can be used in pork, poultry, stuffing and vegetables.

Sumac*

A ground red berry spice that grows wild throughout the Middle East and parts of Italy. Very tart in flavor. Can be used with poultry, vegetables and some lentil dishes.

Zattar*

A native herb to the Middle East. In Arabic it means "thyme" or Syrian marjoram. It is a spice blend composed of toasted sesame seeds, dried thyme, dried marjoram and sumac. Can mix with extra virgin olive oil and salt. Drizzle over bread or use over meats, poultry and vegetables as a seasoning.

Grains and Legumes

Bulgur Wheat

One of the most versatile ingredients in many Middle Eastern dishes. A very nutritious staple that is commonly found in dishes like tabbouleh and kibbi. Can also be used in soups, pilafs and breads. Comes in three different sizes; fine #1, medium #2, and coarse #3 and #4. Use the size according to the recipe requirements.

Chick Peas/ Garbanzo Beans

A huge staple in Mediterranean, Indian and Middle Eastern dishes. It is a legume that is round with a soft texture and chestnut flavor. Very commonly used in hummus, stews, soups, salads and vegetable dishes.

Couscous

A granular semolina/durum hard wheat processed by rolling and steaming. It is a staple in North Africa and the Middle East. It is a compliment to pork, poultry and vegetable dishes.

Lentil (Adas)

Very popular in parts of Europe, India and the Middle East. A perfect substitute for meat. Comes in three varieties. Can be used as a side dish or in soups, salads and stews.

Orzo	A form of barley. Is rice shaped and used in place of rice or pasta. Can be used in a variety of soups.

Seeds and Nuts

Almonds (Loze)	A very nutritious nut. Used widely in Mediterranean countries. They are added to cookies, cakes and many pastries.
Pine Nuts (Snobar)	Come from inside the pinecone. Its torpedo shape is ivory colored. It is very popular in the Middle East for its delicate flavor and versatile uses. Used for topping pastries or fried in butter until light brown and used to garnish rice dishes and in meat and meatless stuffings.
Pistachios (Fustoc Halaby)	Cultivated in California, Turkey, Iran and Italy. Has a hard outside tan shell with a green nut inside. Has a very delicate, subtle flavor that goes well with sweet, savory dishes and pastries.
Sesame Seed (Simsum)	Recorded as the first seasoning. A tiny, flat seed that is commonly found in a variety of colors. Ivory is the most popular. Has a nutty, slightly sweet flavor that is used for baked goods, pastries, salads and savory dishes.

15

| Tahini* | A thick white paste made from crushed raw sesame seeds. Widely used in Middle Eastern cooking. Adds wonderful flavor to a variety of dishes; the most popular and well known is hummus. |

| Walnuts (Jose) | The fruit of the walnut tree that is grown all over the world. Has a meaty taste. A very popular nut for Middle Eastern pastries, such as baklava. |

Miscellaneous Items

| Caper | A native to the Mediterranean. The flower bud is harvested by hand. It is usually pickled or sun-dried. Ranges from a variety of sizes. Adds zest to many salads, meats, poultry or savory dishes. |

| Dates | A native to the Middle East. A fruit that is grown in clusters of a giant date palm tree. The Greeks named it daktulos meaning "finger." The skin is thin and papery. Available fresh or dried. Are used in several Middle Eastern pastries. |

| Feta Cheese | One of the world's oldest cheeses. Has been a product of Greece for many centuries. A crumbly and salty white cheese made from goat's milk. |

Figs	Thought to be sacred as a symbol of peace and prosperity. There are hundreds of varieties and range in colors and sizes. Can be used to flavor cakes, toppings, and pastries.
Filo Dough (Phyllo)	A very popular tissue-thin pastry dough used by Greeks and Middle Eastern countries. The dough is used in sweet and savory preparations. Best known for baklava and spanakopita. Can be purchased fresh or frozen.
Grape Leaves*	Mainly used by the Greek and Middle Eastern countries. Cooks use the leaves to wrap foods for cooking. Well known dishes are grape leaves stuffed with meat and rice (whadda adeesh) or dolmas. You can buy them in jars packed in brine or fresh from a backyard grapevine. If fresh you must simmer them in water for 10 minutes to soften the leaves before wrapping.
Menash*	A wooden handle with short nails making a design to stamp bread or pastry. Used in Middle East baking.
Rose water (Mawarid)*	Rose petals distilled in water to create a perfume fragrance and rose flavor. Adds a wonderful flavor to popular pastries such as baklava and fillings.

Pairing Wine with Food

Wine can be paired with many different dishes. Wine can also be an important element to any dish and food can compliment the wine.

We have showcased different kinds of wines to pair with several recipes. Look for the wine bottle at the bottom of various recipes. Cheers!

Light-bodied, crisp whites	Albarino, Chardonnay (unoaked), Chenin Blanc, Muscadet, Pinot Blanc, Pinot Grigio, White Rioja, Sauvignon Blanc (unoaked), Vinho Verde
Medium-bodied, soft whites	White Bordeaux, Gewurztraminer, Gruner Veltliner, Pinot Gris, Riesling, Sauvignon Blanc (oaked)
Full-bodied, rich whites	White Alsace, White Burgundy, Chardonnay (oaked), Muscat, Roussanne, Semillon, Viognier
Light-bodied, fruity reds	Red Burgundy, Gamay, Nebbiolo, Pinot Noir, Rioja Crianza, Rose'
Medium-bodied, silky reds	Barbera, Cabernet Franc, Chianti, Cotes du Rhone, Dolcetto, Grenache, Malbec, Merlot, Rioja Reserva and Gran Reserva, Sangiovese, Tempranillo
Full-bodied, tannic reds	Barbaresco, Barolo, Red Bordeaux, Brunello, Cabernet Sauvignon, Petite Sirah, Red Rhone, Shiraz/Syrah, Zinfandel
Sparkling wines	Cava, Champagne, Cremant, Prosecco

Appetizers (Mezze)

Festive Green Olive Cheese Ball

Serves 6-8

Ingredients

1 (8 ounce) package cream cheese, softened
1 (8 ounce) package blue cheese, softened
1/4 cup salted butter, softened
2/3 cup green olives with pimentos, chopped
1 tablespoon chives or green onions, chopped
1/2 cup walnuts, pecans, almonds or pistachios, chopped
1/4 cup fresh, flat-leaf parsley, chopped

Method

Blend cheeses and butter together. Stir in olives and chives.
Refrigerate for 1 hour.

Form into a ball and roll in your choice of nuts and parsley.
Place on a serving dish. Chill until firm.

Greek Feta Cheese Spread

Yield 3 cups

Ingredients

1 (8 ounce) package feta cheese, crumbled
2 (8 ounce) packages cream cheese, softened
4 tablespoons kalamata olives, chopped
2 teaspoons garlic, chopped
4 tablespoons extra virgin olive oil
2 teaspoons lemon juice
1 teaspoon dried oregano

Method

Combine all ingredients in a blender or food processor and blend until smooth consistency, scraping sides often.

Chill and serve with fresh raw vegetables, pita bread or pita chips.

Individual Grecian Cheese Balls

Yield 6-8 balls

Ingredients

1/2 cup feta cheese, crumbled
1/2 cup salted butter, softened
1/2 cup kalamata olives, pitted and chopped
2 tablespoons green onions, chopped
1/2 teaspoon paprika

Method

Blend cheese and butter together until a smooth paste. Form into golf ball sized balls. Place olives and onions on separate plates. Roll each cheese ball in the olives, then the green onions. Sprinkle with paprika.

Cover and chill until ready to serve.

Nahima's Syrian Cheese
Rolled in Zattar
(Shunkaleash)

Yield 6-8 balls

Ingredients

1 (4 ounce) package blue cheese
1 (8 ounce) package cream cheese
1 cup salted butter
Red cayenne pepper, to taste
Extra virgin olive oil (for dipping)
1 cup zattar seasoning

Method

Bring cheeses and butter to room temperature. In a bowl, mix together and mash until blended well. Add red cayenne pepper, to taste.

Place mixture in refrigerator. When hard, roll into golf ball size balls. Dip in olive oil, then zattar. Place in a covered container in refrigerator.

Spread on any of your favorite bread or bagel. Also ideal on a cheese tray with crackers.

Greek Olive Tapenade
with Feta Cheese

Serves 6-8

Ingredients

2 ounces feta cheese, crumbled
3 cloves garlic, chopped
2 cups kalamata olives, pitted
1 cup pine nuts
1 cup roasted red peppers, drained
3/4 cup extra virgin olive oil
Salt and pepper, to taste
Dried parsley flakes, for topping

Method

Place all ingredients except olive oil in food processor or blender. Slowly mix, adding oil gradually until a thick paste texture. Store in a covered container. When ready to serve, sprinkle with parsley flakes.

Serve with pita bread, slices of toasted French bread or crackers.

Filo Dough Cups
with Beef and Pinenuts

Yield 30

Ingredients

1 pound ground chuck
2 packages (15 in each) Athenian Mini Filo Shells
1 medium onion, finely chopped
1/4 to 1/2 cup pine nuts
Salt and pepper, to taste
3 tablespoons salted butter

Method

In a saucepan, sauté onion in butter on low until light brown. Add meat, salt, and pepper and cook until brown. Stir in pine nuts and cook an additional 5 minutes on medium-low heat. Drain any oil or liquid.

Remove shells from package. Fill each shell with approximately one teaspoon of meat mixture. Place on an ungreased cookie sheet and bake at 350° for 8-10 minutes or until filo shells are light brown.

Any leftover meat will freeze well and can be used for a Hashwah sandwich inside pita bread. (See Nahima's Pinenuts and Meat Filling (Hashwah) page 131)

Nahima's Simple Stuffed Celery

Serves 4-6

Ingredients

9 celery stalks
1 (8 ounce) package cream cheese, softened
5 tablespoons sweet pickle relish
Paprika, to taste

Method

Wash and trim celery stalks. Remove the leaves and any rough strings. Cut into thirds.

In a mixing bowl, beat cream cheese until smooth. Add sweet pickle relish and mix well. Spoon or pipe cream cheese mixture into the celery stalks. Sprinkle with paprika.

Sauvignon Blanc
(preferably Domestic)

Syrian Bruschetta
with Goat Cheese

Serves 8-10

Ingredients

1 cup Roma tomatoes, seeded and diced
1/4 cup kalamata olives, pitted and chopped
2 tablespoons fresh basil, chopped
1 teaspoon kalamata olive juice (from jar)
1/8 teaspoon salt
1/8 teaspoon ground black pepper
2 loaves French bread baguette, sliced 1/4 inch thick
1/4 cup mild goat cheese, at room temperature
1 clove garlic, peeled

Method

Preheat oven to 400°. In a medium bowl, combine first 6 ingredients. Set aside.

Arrange bread slices on an ungreased baking sheet. Bake for 8 minutes until light brown. Remove toasted bread from oven and cool.

Rub both sides of toast with garlic clove. Spread goat cheese evenly on one side of toast. Top with olive mixture.

Champagne
(preferably Rose')

Baked Pita Chips

Serves 15

Ingredients

8 pita bread rounds
Garlic salt, to taste
Extra virgin olive oil, to taste

Method

Cut pita rounds into triangles. Split in half and place rough side up on an ungreased baking sheet. Sprinkle with garlic salt and drizzle with olive oil.

Bake at 375° for 10 minutes or until brown and crispy. Cool and store in an airtight container.

Serve with any dip.

Can also sprinkle with white sesame seeds or grated Parmesan cheese.

Cucumber Garlic Yogurt Dip

Yield 2 cups

Ingredients

1 (16 ounce) container Greek plain yogurt (store bought)
2 cloves garlic, minced
1/2 teaspoon salt
1/4 teaspoon ground black pepper
2 medium English cucumbers, unpeeled and diced
1 tablespoon dry mint or 2 tablespoons fresh mint, chopped
2 tablespoons extra virgin olive oil

Method

Mix all ingredients together. Refrigerate until ready to serve.
Enjoy with your favorite fresh raw vegetables.

Basic Chickpea Dip
(Hummus)

Yield 3 cups

Ingredients

2 (15 ounce) cans chickpeas, drained, reserving liquid
3-4 tablespoons tahini (more or less, to taste)
5-6 cloves garlic, finely minced
4-5 tablespoons lemon juice
1/3 cup extra virgin olive oil
Salt and pepper, to taste

Method

Combine all ingredients except reserved liquid in a blender or food processor. Slowly add reserved liquid and blend until smooth consistency, scraping sides often.

Place in a medium bowl and garnish with parsley, whole chickpeas, or paprika. Cover with a thin layer of olive oil. Serve with fresh raw vegetables, pita bread, pita chips, tortilla chips or any type of bread cut in cubes.

Sauvignon Blanc
(preferably from New Zealand)

Eggplant Chickpea Dip
with Tahini
(Baba Ghannooj)

Yield 3 cups

Ingredients

1 large eggplant
2 (15 ounce) cans chickpeas, drained, reserving liquid
3-4 tablespoons tahini (more or less, to taste)
4 cloves garlic, finely minced
4-5 tablespoons lemon juice
1/3 cup extra virgin olive oil
Salt and pepper, to taste

Method

Wash and dry eggplant. Slice in rounds. Bake or grill in oven until tender. Peel away skin.

Chop and mash with a fork or food processor.

Place chickpeas, tahini, garlic, lemon juice, and olive oil in blender or food processor adding reserved liquid until smooth consistency. Add eggplant. Add salt and pepper, to taste.

Cover with a thin layer of olive oil. Serve with fresh raw vegetables, pita bread, pita chips, tortilla chips or any type of bread cut in cubes.

Rose'
(preferably Pinot Noir)

Artichoke Chickpea Dip
(Hummus)

Yield 2 cups

Ingredients

1 (15 ounce) can chickpeas, drained reserving liquid
1/2 cup artichoke hearts, drained, chopped
1/4 cup tahini
2 teaspoons garlic, finely minced
4 tablespoons lemon juice
3 tablespoons extra virgin olive oil
Salt and pepper, to taste

Method

Combine all ingredients except reserved liquid in a blender or food processor. Slowly add reserved liquid and blend until smooth consistency, scraping sides often.

Cover with a thin layer of olive oil. Chill and serve with fresh raw vegetables, pita bread or pita chips.

Sauvignon Blanc (preferably New Zealand)
or Gruner Veltliner

Green Chile Chickpea Dip
(Hummus)

Yield 2 cups

Ingredients

1 (15 ounce) can chickpeas, drained, reserving liquid
1 (4 ounce) can diced mild green chilies
1/4 cup tahini
2 teaspoons garlic, finely minced
4 tablespoons lemon juice
3 tablespoons extra virgin olive oil
Salt and pepper, to taste

Method

Combine all ingredients except reserved liquid in a blender or food processor. Slowly add reserved liquid and blend until smooth consistency, scraping sides often.

Cover with a thin layer of olive oil. Chill and serve with fresh raw vegetables, pita bread or pita chips.

Gewurztraminer
(preferably Alsatian)

Hearts of Palm Chickpea Dip
(Hummus)

Yield 2 cups

Ingredients

1 (15 ounce) can chickpeas, drained, reserving liquid
1 (14 ounce) can hearts of palm, drained
1/4 cup tahini
2 teaspoons garlic, finely minced
4 tablespoons lemon juice
3 tablespoons extra virgin olive oil
Salt and pepper, to taste

Method

Combine all ingredients except reserved liquid in a blender or food processor. Slowly add reserved liquid and blend until smooth consistency, scraping sides often.

Cover with a thin layer of olive oil. Chill and serve with fresh raw vegetables, pita bread or pita chips.

Jalapeno Chickpea Dip
(Hummus)

Yield 2 cups

Ingredients

1 (15 ounce) can chickpeas, drained, reserving liquid
1/2 cup jalapeno peppers, seeded and finely minced
1/4 cup tahini
2 teaspoons garlic, finely minced
4 tablespoons lemon juice
3 tablespoons extra virgin olive oil
Salt and pepper, to taste

Method

Combine all ingredients except reserved liquid in a blender or food processor. Slowly add reserved liquid and blend until smooth consistency, scraping sides often.

Cover with a thin layer of olive oil. Chill and serve with fresh raw vegetables, pita bread or pita chips.

Pinot Gris
(preferably Oregon)

Sun-dried Tomato Chickpea Dip

(Hummus)

Yield 2 cups

Ingredients

1 (15 ounce) can chickpeas, drained, reserving liquid
1/2 cup sun-dried tomatoes, finely chopped
1/4 cup tahini
2 teaspoons garlic, finely minced
1 teaspoon ground cumin
4 tablespoons lemon juice
3 tablespoons extra virgin olive oil
Salt and pepper, to taste

Method

Combine all ingredients except reserved liquid in a blender or food processor. Slowly add reserved liquid and blend until smooth consistency, scraping sides often.

Cover with a thin layer of olive oil. Chill and serve with fresh raw vegetables, pita bread or pita chips.

Albarino

Sweet Caramelized Onion Chickpea Dip
(Hummus)

Yield 2 cups

Ingredients

1 (15 ounce) can chickpeas, drained, reserving liquid
1 medium onion, chopped
1/4 cup tahini
2 teaspoons garlic, finely minced
4 tablespoons lemon juice
3 tablespoons extra virgin olive oil
Salt and pepper, to taste

Method

In a sauté pan, heat 1 tablespoon of olive oil over medium heat. Add onions and garlic and cook 10-12 minutes, stirring occasionally, until brown. Remove from heat.

Combine all ingredients in a blender or food processor. Slowly add reserved liquid and blend until smooth consistency, scraping sides often.

Cover with a thin layer of olive oil. Chill and serve with fresh raw vegetables, pita bread or pita chips.

Pinot Gris, Alsatian

Roasted Red Pepper Chickpea Dip
(Hummus)

Yield 2 cups

Ingredients

1 (15 ounce) can chickpeas, drained, reserving liquid
1/2 cup roasted red peppers, drained and chopped
1/4 cup tahini
2 teaspoons garlic, finely minced
1 teaspoon ground cumin
4 tablespoons lemon juice
3 tablespoons extra virgin olive oil
Salt and pepper, to taste

Method

Combine all ingredients except reserved liquid in a blender or food processor. Slowly add reserved liquid and blend until smooth consistency, scraping sides often.

Cover with a thin layer of olive oil. Chill and serve with fresh raw vegetables, pita bread or pita chips.

> *Viognier, Semillon or*
> *Rose' (preferably Spanish)*

Glorious Chickpea Dip
with Green Olives
(Hummus)

Yield 2 cups

Ingredients

1 (15 ounce) can chickpeas, drained, reserving liquid
4 cloves garlic, finely minced
1/4 cup tahini
1/4 cup green olives with pimentos
1/2 teaspoon ground cumin
4 teaspoons lemon juice
3 tablespoons extra virgin olive oil
Salt and pepper, to taste

Method

Place all ingredients in a food processor except reserved liquid. Blend well until thick and chunky. If you like it smoother, add reserved liquid. Serve with fresh raw vegetables, crackers or pita bread.

Andrea's Exotic Black Bean and Chickpea Dip
(Hummus)

Serves 4-6

Ingredients

1 (15 ounce) can chickpeas, drained, reserving liquid
1 (15 ounce) can black beans, drained, rinsed
3 cloves garlic, finely minced
1/2 cup lemon juice
1/2 cup tahini
4 tablespoons extra virgin olive oil
Paprika, to taste
Salt and pepper, to taste

Method

In a food processor or blender, puree chickpeas, black beans, and garlic with some of the chickpea liquid until smooth, about 2 minutes. Add lemon juice, tahini, olive oil, salt and pepper. Blend well. If too thick, add more chickpea liquid to desired consistency. Garnish with paprika.

Serve with fresh raw vegetables of your choice or pita bread.

Tex-Mex Chickpea Dip
(Hummus)

Yield 2 cups

Ingredients

1 (15 ounce) can chickpeas, drained, reserving liquid
1 (1.25 ounce) package taco seasoning mix, sprinkle to taste
1/4 cup tahini
2 teaspoons garlic, finely minced
2 green onions, finely chopped
4 tablespoons lemon juice
3 tablespoons extra virgin olive oil
Salt and pepper, to taste
Cheddar cheese, grated, for garnish (about 2 tablespoons)

Method

Combine all ingredients except cheddar cheese in a blender or food processor and blend until smooth consistency, scraping sides often. Add reserved liquid to desired consistency.

Sprinkle with cheddar cheese. Chill and serve with fresh raw vegetables, pita bread or pita chips.

Savory Roasted Chickpeas

Yield 2 cups

Ingredients

1 (15 ounce) can chickpeas, drained and rinsed
2 tablespoons extra virgin olive oil
1 tablespoon balsamic vinegar
3 cloves garlic, chopped
1/2 teaspoon sea salt

Method

In a small bowl, toss all ingredients together and put in a single layer on an ungreased baking sheet. Bake at 400° until crunchy or desired taste. Can add to salads.

Riesling
(preferably off-dry)

Mediterranean Pickled Olives

Yield 1 pint

Ingredients

1 (5 3/4 ounce) can green olives, pitted, drained
1 teaspoon dried oregano
1/4 teaspoon crushed red pepper flakes
1 clove garlic, minced
1/4 teaspoon onion, chopped
1/2 cup red wine or balsamic vinegar
1/4 cup extra virgin olive oil

Method

In a pint size jar, pack olives first, then liquid. Add remaining ingredients. Cover with lid and shake well. Keep in the refrigerator for three days or more before serving.

Herb Marinated Olives

Ingredients

Variety of olives:
Kalamata
Manzanilla
Castelventrano
Greek black
Picholine
Nicoise

Extra virgin olive oil
Dried rosemary
Dried thyme
Crushed red pepper
Lemon zest to taste
Sea salt and pepper, to taste

Method

Use your own creativity to design your own taste, without measurements.

In an airtight container or jar, drizzle olives with olive oil. Add remaining ingredients. Mix together and chill until ready to serve.

Traditional Yogurt
(Laban)

Ingredients

1 quart whole milk
1 tablespoon plain yogurt (as starter), (store bought)

Method

Heat milk in a saucepan on low heat until milk comes to a boil. Remove pan from heat and let cool to lukewarm.

In a glass bowl, add 2 tablespoons of warm milk to the yogurt and stir until smooth. Pour the rest of the milk in the bowl and stir.

Cover with plastic wrap, then a heavy cloth or blanket. Store in a warm place for about 5 hours. Mixture will thicken like custard.

When thickened, put in refrigerator in an airtight container.

Laban is used many different ways. It can be eaten with baked kibbi, on toast or pita bread, or can be used as a dip for fresh raw vegetables.

Can also add salt, pepper and extra virgin olive oil, to taste.

Creamy Cream Cheese
(Labneh)

Ingredients

Traditional Yogurt recipe

Method

Make Traditional Yogurt according to recipe. Transfer yogurt to a cheesecloth. Gently squeeze out juices. Tie with a rubber band to close the top. Drain in a small colander and bowl to reduce the liquid. Keep in the refrigerator for a day until thick like cream cheese.

Remove cheesecloth and put all the cheese in an airtight container. Cover with extra virgin olive oil to preserve.

Can add any seasonings or spices for extra flavor.

Can serve with bread, as a dip for fresh raw vegetables, or with any sandwich as a condiment.

Contemporary Yogurt
(Laban)

Ingredients

1 (16 ounce) container plain yogurt, (store bought)
Extra virgin olive oil, to taste

Method

Pour yogurt from container into a cheesecloth. Gently squeeze out liquid. Place in a colander and bowl. Let drain in the refrigerator for a few days until liquid is removed. Take out and add extra virgin olive oil on top to preserve. Lasts a couple of weeks in the refrigerator.

Can add any seasonings or spices for extra flavor.

Can serve with bread, used as a dip for fresh raw vegetables, or with any sandwich as a condiment.

Salads, Dressings & Marinades

Basic Oil and Vinegar Dressing or Marinade

Yield 1 quart

Ingredients

3 cups extra virgin olive oil
1 cup red wine vinegar
4 teaspoons Dijon mustard
2 teaspoons sugar or honey
2 teaspoons salt
1 teaspoon ground black pepper

Method

Mix all ingredients in a jar; shake well. Store in refrigerator to use as a salad dressing, on steamed vegetables, or as a marinade for chicken, pork or fish.

Can also add fresh chopped herbs for extra flavor.

Garlic and Dijon Mustard Dressing or Marinade

Yield 1 1/4 cups

Ingredients

1 cup extra virgin olive oil
1/4 cup red wine vinegar
1 teaspoon Dijon mustard
1 teaspoon ground black pepper

Method

Mix all ingredients in a jar; shake well. Store in refrigerator to use as a salad dressing, or as a marinade for chicken or fish.

Can also pour over 1 (16 ounce) package coleslaw mix.

Greek Salad Dressing
with Feta Cheese

Yield 1 1/2 cups

Ingredients

1 (8 ounce) package feta cheese, crumbled
1 cup extra virgin olive oil
1/3 cup red wine vinegar

Method

Place feta cheese in a food processor or blender. Slowly add oil and vinegar, alternating, until desired consistency. Blend well. Refrigerate until ready to use.

Can be used on salad, over cooked vegetables, grilled chicken, or coleslaw mix.

Mediterranean Basic Salad Dressing

Yield 1 1/2 cups

Ingredients

3/4 cup extra virgin olive oil
1/2 cup lemon juice
3 cloves garlic, minced
1/2 teaspoon salt
1/4 teaspoon ground black pepper

Method

In a medium bowl, mash garlic into salt. Add remaining ingredients and place in a jar. Cover and shake.

Keep in refrigerator until needed. You can also marinate vegetables and poultry in a zip-lock bag in the refrigerator.

add a wee bit of sweetener

Tahini Dressing
with Garlic and Parsley

Yield 3 cups

Ingredients

1 cup tahini
1 cup lemon juice
1 1/2 cups fresh, flat-leaf parsley, coarsely chopped
1 teaspoon salt
1/2 teaspoon ground black pepper
4 cloves garlic, minced
1/2 cup cold water

Method

Alternating ingredients in small amounts, combine lemon juice water and tahini in a blender or food processor. Add garlic, salt and pepper. Place in a bowl and blend in parsley. Place in jar or airtight container and keep chilled in refrigerator until needed.

Pour over any salad, steamed vegetables, or as an accompaniment for meat, fish or chicken dish.

Tahini Sauce
with Parsley

Yield 3 cups

Ingredients

1 1/2 cups fresh, flat-leaf parsley, chopped
1 cup tahini
1 cup lemon juice
3 cloves garlic, chopped
1 1/4 teaspoons salt
1/4 teaspoon ground black pepper
1/2 cup cold water

Method

Mix tahini, salt, pepper, lemon juice and garlic in a blender. Add parsley at low speed. Do not overblend. Slowly add cold water until smooth, but not runny. Serve over fish, chicken or meat.

Cucumber and Yogurt Salad

Serves 4-6

Ingredients

2 cups Greek plain yogurt, (store bought)
1 English cucumber, unpeeled, cut in small cubes
1 clove garlic, minced
1 teaspoon dried mint
1 teaspoon extra virgin olive oil
Salt and pepper, to taste

Method

Mix all ingredients together in a bowl. Store in refrigerator until ready to serve.

Nahima's Fresh Avocado Salad

Serves 4

Ingredients

2 small California avocados
Extra virgin olive oil, to taste
1 teaspoon lemon juice
1 clove garlic, pressed
Salt and pepper, to taste

Method

Slice avocado in half. Remove seed. Score the inside horizontally, then vertically. Scoop out with a spoon and place in a bowl. Drizzle with olive oil. Add salt, pepper, lemon juice and garlic. Toss gently. Chill and serve.

Greek Chickpea Salad

Serves 6-8

Ingredients

2 (15 ounce) cans chickpeas, drained and rinsed
1/4 cup celery, chopped
1/4 cup onions, chopped
1/4 cup vinegar of your choice
3/4 cup extra virgin olive oil
2 cloves garlic, minced
1/4 teaspoon paprika
1/4 teaspoon ground black pepper
1/2 teaspoon salt
1/2 teaspoon dried oregano
2 tablespoons dried parsley
1/2 cup feta cheese, crumbled

Method

In a large bowl, mix together oil, vinegar, herbs and spices. Add celery, onions, and chickpeas. Toss gently. Top with feta cheese.

Chill for several hours. Serve cold on a bed of greens.

Lebanese Salad
(Salata)

Serves 6-8

Ingredients

1 head romaine lettuce
1 head iceberg lettuce
3 medium tomatoes, chopped
1 small onion, chopped
1/2 bunch green onions, chopped
5-6 tablespoons fresh, flat-leaf parsley, chopped
3-4 tablespoons fresh mint, chopped, or 1 tablespoon dry mint
2 small cucumbers, peeled and cubed
1/2 small green bell pepper, cubed

Dressing:
1/4 cup extra virgin olive oil
1/4 cup canola oil
3 tablespoons lemon juice
1 teaspoon salt
1/2 teaspoon ground black pepper
1 tablespoon white vinegar
1 clove garlic, minced

Method

Wash lettuce, dry, and chop in chunks. Place in refrigerator to chill. In a large salad bowl, place remaining ingredients, then top with chilled lettuce. Pour dressing over lettuce and toss gently.

Simple Cabbage Salad

Serves 4-6

Ingredients

1/2 small head green cabbage, washed and cut into chunks
2 cloves garlic, pressed
1/4 cup lemon juice
1/4 cup extra virgin olive oil
Salt and pepper, to taste
Poppy seeds, to taste (optional)

Method

In a jar, mix juice, oil, garlic, salt and pepper. Shake well. Pour over chopped cabbage in a bowl and toss. Sprinkle with poppy seeds.

Syrian Style Salad

Serves 4-6

Ingredients

1 bunch escarole or endive lettuce, washed and dried
3 medium tomatoes, chopped
1 cucumber, peeled
Juice of 1 lemon
3 cloves garlic, minced
1/4 cup extra virgin olive oil
Salt and pepper, to taste

Method

Tear lettuce into bite-sized pieces. Place in large salad bowl. Add tomatoes. Cut cucumbers into 4 sticks, then slice into 1/2 inch pieces. Place lemon juice, garlic, olive oil, salt and pepper in a jar with a lid. Shake well. Pour over the lettuce, tomatoes and cucumbers. Toss gently and serve immediately.

Tangy Chickpea Salad

Serves 2

Ingredients

1 (15 ounce) can chickpeas, drained and rinsed
2 cloves garlic, pressed
1/2 teaspoon salt
1/2 teaspoon ground black pepper
Extra virgin olive oil, to taste
Lemon juice, to taste
1 teaspoon dried parsley
   or 2 tablespoons fresh, flat-leaf parsley, chopped

Method

In a small bowl, combine all ingredients. Mix well. Refrigerate until chilled.

Vegetable Lover's Salad

Serves 6-8

Ingredients

1 medium green cabbage, shredded
2 English cucumbers, unpeeled, thinly sliced
1 large red onion, thinly sliced into rings
1 cup celery, diced
2 carrots, sliced in rounds
1/2 red bell pepper, seeded and diced
1/2 green bell pepper, seeded and diced
1/2 cup radishes, sliced in rounds
3/4 cup red wine vinegar
1/4 cup water
3/4 cup sugar
1/4 cup extra virgin olive oil
1 teaspoon salt
1/2 teaspoon ground black pepper

Method

In a large bowl, combine all vegetables. In a jar, mix remaining ingredients. Shake well until sugar is dissolved. Pour over vegetables. Mix well. Refrigerate until chilled.

Hearts of Palm and Artichoke Salad

Serves 4

Ingredients

1 (15 ounce) can artichoke hearts, (cut in quarters), drained
1 (15 ounce) can hearts of palm (cut in 1/2" rounds), drained
2 garlic cloves, pressed
2 tablespoons extra virgin olive oil
Juice of 1 lemon
2 tablespoons fresh, flat-leaf parsley, chopped

Method

In a bowl, place artichokes and hearts of palm. Add remaining ingredients. Mix well. Refrigerate until ready to serve.

Delicious Couscous Salad

Serves 8

Ingredients

1 cup English cucumber, unpeeled, diced
1 cup tomatoes, diced
1 cup green onions, chopped
1 cup fresh, flat-leaf parsley, chopped
1/4 teaspoon ground black pepper
1/2 cup extra virgin olive oil
3/4 cup lemon juice
3 cloves garlic, pressed
1 teaspoon salt
1 teaspoon dry mint
1 cup cooked couscous

Method

In a bowl, mix all ingredients together. Chill in refrigerator until ready to serve.

Greek God Couscous Salad

Serves 8

Ingredients

1 cup cooked couscous
1/2 cup feta cheese, crumbled
1 cup tomatoes, diced
1 cup English cucumber, unpeeled, diced
1 cup green onions, chopped
1 cup green bell pepper, diced (can also used red or yellow)
1/4 teaspoon ground black pepper
1 teaspoon salt
1 teaspoon dried mint
1/2 cup extra virgin olive oil
3/4 cup lemon juice
3 cloves garlic, pressed
1/2 cup black olives, pitted and chopped

Method

In a bowl, mix all ingredients together. Chill in refrigerator until ready to serve.

Mediterranean Potato Salad

Serves 8-10

Ingredients

3 pounds white potatoes
1 cup fresh, flat-leaf parsley, chopped
1/2 cup fresh mint, chopped or 1 tablespoon dried mint
1 large onion or 1 bunch green onions, chopped
1/2 cup extra virgin olive oil
1/3 cup lemon juice
1 teaspoon salt
1/2 teaspoon ground black pepper
2 cloves garlic, minced
2/3 cup green olives with pimentos, chopped
Paprika, to taste

Method

Boil potatoes. Cool and peel. Dice potatoes and place in large
bowl. Add remaining ingredients except olives and paprika.
Mix well. Chill before serving. Garnish with olives and
paprika.

Mouthwatering Vegetable Salad
with Toasted Pita Bread
(Fattoush)

Serves 8

Ingredients

2 rounds of pita bread
2 cucumbers, peeled and diced
2 pounds ripe tomatoes, chopped
1 bunch green onions, chopped
1 bunch fresh, flat-leaf parsley, chopped
1 tablespoon dried mint or 1 bunch fresh mint, chopped

Dressing:

1/2 cup lemon juice
1 clove garlic pressed
1 cup extra virgin olive oil
1/2 tablespoon salt
1 teaspoon ground black pepper
1 tablespoon zattar seasoning

Method

Toast pita bread on rack in 300° oven until light brown. Cool and break into pieces.

In a bowl, combine all vegetables and herbs. Add toasted pita chips. Pour dressing over all ingredients and toss to mix. Serve immediately.

Can add chopped dill pickles, artichoke hearts or hearts of palm.

Chopped Chickpea Salad

Serves 4-6

Ingredients

3 (15 ounce) cans chickpeas, drained and rinsed
2 medium green bell peppers, chopped
2 medium red onions, chopped
1 cup extra virgin olive oil
1 teaspoon garlic powder
1/2 teaspoon dried cumin
1/2 teaspoon dried oregano
Salt and pepper, to taste

Method

In a large bowl, combine all ingredients. Toss well and chill until ready to serve.

Della's Wheat and Parsley Salad
(Tabbouleh)

Serves 4-6

Ingredients

1 cup #2 bulgur wheat
1 bunch green onions, chopped
3 medium tomatoes, diced
1 bunch fresh, curly parsley, chopped
8 leaves of romaine lettuce, washed and dried
2 tablespoons fresh mint, chopped (optional)
1/4 cup lemon juice
1/4 cup extra virgin olive oil
Salt and pepper, to taste

Method

Place bulgur wheat in a bowl and cover with cold water. Let soak for 20 minutes. Drain excess water if necessary. In another bowl, combine tomatoes, green onions and mint. Add wheat and mix well.

Fill each romaine leaf with parsley leaves. Roll and cut. Add to bowl with vegetables. Add oil, seasonings and lemon juice. Mix well.

Serve chilled. Can be eaten inside pita bread or in fresh lettuce leaves.

Greek Wheat and Parsley Salad
with Feta Cheese
(Tabbouleh)

Serves 8-10

Ingredients

1 cup #2 bulgur wheat
1/3 cup lemon juice
3 tablespoons extra virgin olive oil
1 bunch green onions, chopped
1 small red onion, chopped
1 cucumber, peeled and chopped
2 large tomatoes, chopped
1 clove garlic, pressed
1 cup fresh, flat-leaf parsley, chopped
2 tablespoons dry mint or 1/3 cup fresh mint, chopped
1/4 teaspoon salt
1/4 teaspoon pepper
1/2 cup feta cheese, crumbled

Method

In a bowl, place bulgur wheat and cover with cold water. Let soak for 20 minutes. Drain excess water if necessary.

Place all ingredients in another bowl and mix with wheat. Top with feta cheese. Refrigerate until ready to serve.

Nahima's Traditional Wheat and Parsley Salad
(Tabbouleh)

Serves 6

Ingredients

3/4 cup #1 fine bulgur wheat
3/4 cup green onions, finely chopped ,
1/4 cup fresh mint, chopped (optional)
2 cups fresh, curly parsley, chopped in food processor
2 medium tomatoes, chopped
1/4 cup lemon juice
1/4 cup extra virgin olive oil
Salt and pepper, to taste
Black olives for garnish

Method

In a bowl, place bulgur wheat and cover with cold water. Let soak for 20 minutes. Drain excess water if necessary.

In another bowl, mix together onion, mint, parsley, tomatoes, seasonings, oil, and lemon juice.

Tabbouleh should have a distinctive lemony flavor. Serve chilled, in a glass dish decorated with a few black olives.

Tabbouleh can be eaten scooped up in bread or more traditionally in fresh lettuce leaves.

Colorful Contemporary Wheat and Parsley Salad
(Tabbouleh)

Serves 8-10

Ingredients

1 cup #2 bulgur wheat
1/4 cup English cucumber, unpeeled, diced
1/4 cup green onions, finely chopped
1/4 cup tomatoes, diced
1/4 cup radishes, chopped
3/4 cup fresh, curly parsley, chopped
3/4 cup fresh mint, chopped
1/4 cup lemon juice
1/4 cup extra virgin olive oil
Salt, pepper and garlic powder, to taste

Method

In a bowl, place bulgur wheat and cover with cold water. Let soak for 20 minutes. Drain excess water if necessary.

In another bowl, place vegetables. Mix well. Add bulgur wheat, olive oil, lemon juice, salt, pepper, and garlic powder. Serve chilled.

Soups & Stews

Nahima's Syrian Soup
with Cabbage
(Kibbi Kisch)

Serves 6-8

Ingredients

2 pounds ground round
1 large head green cabbage, chopped
2 cups #2 bulgur wheat, rinsed, not soaked
1 1/2 cups kisch seasoning
1/2 cup salted butter
Salt and pepper, to taste

Method

In a large pot, place cabbage with enough water to cover. Cover and cook until tender.

In a small bowl, combine kisch and 1 cup hot water. Let stand for 30 minutes or more until it rises. Add to the cabbage, stirring well. Continue to cook on medium-low heat.

In another bowl, combine beef and wheat. Mix well and knead together. Add salt and pepper and continue to mix. Form a golf ball size ball of kibbi. Cut the butter into 1/2" pieces. Place a piece of butter in the center of each ball. Pinch the top to close. Add kibbi balls to the cabbage. Cook on high until it comes to a boil. Reduce heat, cover and cook on medium-low heat for 20 minutes or until kibbi is done. Serve hot.

Multi-colored Mediterranean Bean Soup

Serves 6-8

Ingredients

1 (15 ounce) can dark kidney beans, drained
1 (15 ounce) can black beans, drained
1 (15 ounce) can black eyed peas, drained
1 (15 ounce) can chickpeas, drained
1/2 cup long-grain white rice, washed and drained, uncooked
1/2 cup dried lentils, washed and drained
1 large onion, chopped
4 cloves garlic, chopped
6 cups chicken or beef broth
1/2 cup extra virgin olive oil
Salt and pepper, to taste

Method

In a large soup pot, bring broth to a boil. Add rice and lentils. Cook until tender.

In a saucepan, sauté onions and garlic in olive oil until light brown. Add to rice and lentils. Add all the beans, salt and pepper. Simmer uncovered until done.

Savory Lentil Soup

Serves 4-6

Ingredients

2 cups dried lentils, rinsed and drained
8 cups chicken broth
2 cloves garlic, minced
1 medium onion, chopped
1/4 cup extra virgin olive oil
Salt and pepper, to taste

Method

In a large soup pot, Boil lentils until tender, about 30 minutes on medium heat. In a skillet, heat oil and sauté onions, garlic, salt and pepper. Pour onion and garlic mixture into the lentils and cook another 15 minutes until done.

Comfort Heartwarming Soup
with Chickpeas
(Yahnee)

Serves 4-6

Ingredients

4 boneless, skinless chicken breasts, cubed
3 medium onions, chopped
4 carrots, peeled and sliced in 1/2" rounds
3 celery stalks, chopped
1 (15 ounce) can chickpeas, drained
3 tablespoons salted butter
Salt and pepper, to taste

Method

In a large soup pot, melt butter and sauté onions until tender. Add chicken and continue to cook until brown. Add more butter if necessary.

Add carrots, celery, salt and pepper. Mix together. Add enough water to cover. Bring to a boil. Reduce heat and cover. Simmer for 45 minutes or until chicken and vegetables are tender. During the last 5 minutes, add chickpeas and stir well. Serve hot.

Sauvignon Blanc

Papa's Columbian Soup
(Puchero)

Serves 6-8

Ingredients

2 pounds beef chuck roast
1/2 large head of green cabbage, quartered
6 carrots, cut in 6 pieces
4 medium white potatoes, peeled and quartered
2 medium turnips, peeled and quartered
1 large onion, quartered
2 cloves garlic, cut in half
1 (14.5 ounce) can petite or diced tomatoes, undrained
Salt and pepper, to taste

Method

Trim fat from beef and cut into cubes. Place 6 cups of water into large soup pot. Add beef cubes, garlic, onion, salt and pepper. Cover and bring to a boil. Skim off fat. Reduce to low and simmer for 1 hour until meat is tender.

Add remaining ingredients. Bring to a boil. Reduce to medium and cook until vegetables are done.

Serve with crusty bread.

Beaujolais

Chicken and Vegetable Soup
with Orzo and Chickpeas

Serves 6

Ingredients

2 cups cooked chicken breast, shredded
1 cup orzo pasta, uncooked
3 carrots, peeled and sliced in 1/2" rounds
2 celery stalks, sliced in 1/2" rounds
2 medium onions, chopped
1 (15 ounce) can chickpeas, drained
3 cloves garlic, chopped
7 cups chicken broth
Salt and pepper, to taste
Dried parsley for garnish

Method

In a large soup pot, bring broth to a boil. Add orzo; reduce heat to low; cover and simmer about 15 minutes, stirring occasionally until orzo is tender. Stir in remaining ingredients. Cover and simmer for an additional 30 minutes until vegetables are tender.

Garnish with parsley.

Chicken and Lentil Soup
with Squash and Zucchini

Serves 6

Ingredients

1 pound boneless, skinless chicken breasts, cut into pieces
2 medium yellow squash, chopped
2 medium zucchini, chopped
3 carrots, peeled and chopped
1 (14 ounce) can diced tomatoes, undrained
2 cloves garlic, chopped
1 cup dried lentils, drained and rinsed
4 1/2 cups chicken broth
Parmesan cheese, grated, for garnish

Method

In a large soup pot, bring chicken broth to boil. Add chicken and simmer on low until chicken is tender. Add remaining ingredients. Cook until vegetables are tender, about 30 minutes.

Top with grated Parmesan cheese.

Chardonnay or Chenin Blanc

Summer Shrimp Stew
with White Wine

Serves 4-6

Ingredients

2 pounds medium raw shrimp, peeled, deveined
1 large onion, chopped
2 cloves garlic, chopped
2 carrots, chopped
2 tablespoons flour
4 tablespoons salted butter
4 medium ripe tomatoes, chopped
1 (8 ounce) can tomato sauce
1/4 cup white wine
Salt and pepper, to taste

Method

In a large pan, sauté onions, garlic and carrots in butter until light brown. Add raw shrimp and stir over low heat until light brown. Gradually add flour and stir until blended.

Add tomatoes, tomato sauce, white wine, salt and pepper. Continue cooking about 30 minutes uncovered or until done. Serve with any rice, couscous or grain dish.

Muscadet

Chickpea and Eggplant Stew
(Batinjoan)

Serves 4

Ingredients

1 medium eggplant, peeled, chopped
1 cup onion, chopped
2 (14.5 ounce) cans diced tomatoes, undrained
2 (15 ounce) cans chickpeas, drained
1 1/2 teaspoon salt
1/4 teaspoon ground black pepper
4 tablespoons extra virgin olive oil

Method

In a large skillet, heat olive oil; sauté onions until tender. Add eggplant and sauté another 10 minutes, stirring occasionally. Stir in salt, pepper, tomatoes and chickpeas. Cover and cook over low heat for 30 minutes.

Can serve over Elegant Mediterranean Rice. (see recipe page 81)

Crisp Okra Stew
with Beef
(Bamee)

Serves 4

Ingredients

1 pound lean ground chuck
1 pound frozen or fresh okra, sliced in rounds
1 clove garlic, minced
1 large onion, chopped
2 (14.5 ounce) can diced tomatoes, undrained
2 tablespoons lemon juice
3 tablespoons extra virgin olive oil
Salt and pepper, to taste

Method

In a pan, sauté okra in olive oil until tender; set aside.

In another pan, sauté beef until brown. Add onions and garlic. Simmer until tender. Add tomatoes and continue to simmer 30 minutes.

Add okra and lemon juice. Continue cooking for 15 minutes.

Serve over Elegant Mediterranean Rice (see recipe page 81)

Rice, Grains, & Legumes

Elegant Mediterranean Rice

Serves 4

Ingredients

1 cup long-grain white rice, uncooked
2 cups chicken broth
2 1/2 tablespoons salted butter
1 teaspoon salt
2 tablespoons spaghetti, broken into 1/2 inch pieces

Method

In a saucepan, melt butter over medium heat and sauté spaghetti until light brown. Add broth, rice and salt. Bring to a boil. Reduce heat to low; cover tightly and simmer for 20 minutes. Serve as a side dish.

Refreshing Lemony Rice
with Pine Nuts

Serves 6

Ingredients

1 1/2 cups long-grain white rice, uncooked
3 cups chicken broth
3 tablespoons salted butter
1/4 cup pine nuts, toasted
1/4 cup lemon juice
2 green onions, finely chopped
Salt and pepper, to taste

Method

In a saucepan, bring broth and rice to a boil. Add remaining ingredients. Reduce heat to low and cover. Simmer for 20 minutes. Remove from heat and set aside until all liquid is absorbed and rice is tender. Serve as a side dish.

Fragrant Meatless Rice
with Spices

Serves 4-6

Ingredients

2 cups long-grain white rice, uncooked
1/2 cup pine nuts, toasted
1 cup onions, chopped
1/4 cup extra virgin olive oil
1 teaspoon salt
1/8 teaspoon ground cinnamon
1/8 teaspoon allspice
4 cups chicken broth

Method

In a large saucepan, sauté pine nuts in oil. Remove from pan and set aside.

In same pan, sauté onions in oil until light brown. Add rice and salt to oil and sauté for a few minutes. Pour broth into pan. Add cinnamon and allspice. Mix well. Bring to a boil; cover with a lid and reduce heat to low and simmer for 20 minutes or until broth is completely absorbed.

When completed, turn out rice onto a platter and sprinkle pine nuts on top.

Spicy Tomato Rice

Serves 4

Ingredients

1 cup long-grain white rice, uncooked
1 small onion, chopped
2 cloves garlic, minced
1 (8 ounce) can tomato sauce
3/4 teaspoon salt
1/3 teaspoon ground black pepper
1/3 teaspoon allspice
3 tablespoons extra virgin olive oil
2 cups water or vegetable broth

Method

In a saucepan, sauté onions and garlic in oil until tender, not brown.

In another saucepan, place water or broth and tomato sauce and bring to a boil. Add rice, onions, garlic and spices. Stir, cover and simmer on low heat for 30 minutes or until rice is very tender and juice is absorbed.

Serve as a side dish.

*Gewurztraminer, Barbera
or Sangiovese (preferably New World)*

Middle East Pilaf

Serves 4-6

Ingredients

1 cup long grain rice, uncooked
2 cups beef broth
2 tablespoons salted butter
1 medium onion, chopped
1/4 cup raisins
1/2 cup almonds, sliced
2 tablespoons fresh, flat-leaf parsley, chopped

Method

In a saucepan, melt butter and sauté onion until tender. Add broth, raisins, almonds, parsley and rice. Stir well.

Bring to a boil, then reduce heat. Cover and simmer for 20 minutes.

Serve as a side dish.

Tender Orzo and Rice

Serves 2-4

Ingredients

2 tablespoons salted butter
2 cups chicken broth
1 cup long-grain white rice, uncooked
2 tablespoons orzo pasta, uncooked
1 teaspoon salt

Method

In a saucepan, melt butter and sauté orzo until light brown. Add broth, rice and salt.

Bring to a boil. Reduce heat to low and simmer for 15 minutes or until broth is absorbed.

Serve as a side dish.

Lemony Orzo

Serves 4-6

Ingredients

6 cups water
1 cup orzo pasta, uncooked
1/4 teaspoon saffron, crushed
2 teaspoons fresh lemon zest
2 tablespoons lemon juice
3 tablespoons extra virgin olive oil
3 green onions, finely chopped
1 tablespoon dried parsley
Salt, to taste

Method

In a medium saucepan, bring water and saffron to a boil. Add orzo and continue to boil for 8 minutes or until orzo is al dente. Drain and set aside.

In a medium bowl, combine lemon zest, lemon juice and salt to taste. Slowly add olive oil and whisk gently to blend. Add green onions and parsley.

Toss the cooked orzo into the bowl. Serve at room temperature.

Plain and Simple Couscous

Serves 6

Ingredients

1 1/2 cups couscous, uncooked
2 1/2 cups water or chicken broth
1/4 teaspoon salt

Method

In a saucepan, bring water or broth to a boil. Stir in salt and add couscous. Remove immediately from heat and let stand for 5 minutes to absorb water. Fluff with a fork before serving.

Couscous should be fluffy and light, not sticky or gummy. Serve hot or cold.

For a variety, add your favorite diced vegetables and herbs for a flavorful dish.

Spicy Couscous

Serves 6

Ingredients

1 1/2 cups couscous, uncooked
2 1/2 cups chicken broth
2 teaspoons paprika
2 cloves garlic, minced
1 tablespoon lemon juice
1/4 teaspoon cayenne pepper
5 green onions, finely chopped
3 tablespoons extra virgin olive oil

Method

In a saucepan, combine all ingredients. Bring to boil; stir once; turn off heat and let stand for 5 minutes.

When completely done, fluff with a fork and serve hot.

Dilly of a Bulgur Dish

Serves 4

Ingredients

1 medium onion, chopped
1/2 stick butter
1 teaspoon salt
1/2 teaspoon ground black pepper
1 teaspoon dried dill weed
1 cups #3 bulgur wheat
2 cups chicken broth

Method

In a saucepan, melt butter. Add onion and cook until tender. Add bulgur, broth and spices. Bring to a boil; cover and reduce heat to a simmer.

Cook on low for 20 minutes. Serve with any entree.

Baked Middle Eastern Chickpea and Bulgur Wheat

Serves 8-10

Ingredients

1/4 cup salted butter
1 medium onion, chopped
1 1/2 cups #2 or #3 bulgur wheat
2 1/2 cups chicken broth
1/4 cup chickpeas, drained
Non-stick cooking spray

Method

Preheat oven to 350°.

In a saucepan, melt butter and sauté the onion until tender. Add chicken broth and wheat and stir until mixture boils. Add chickpeas.

Pour into a baking dish which has been lightly sprayed with non-stick cooking spray. Cover and bake for 20 minutes.

Remove from oven, stir, cover and return to oven for an additional 20-30 minutes.

Lentils, Black-eyed Peas and Bulgur Wheat
(Mujadara)

Serves 6-8

Ingredients

1 cup dried lentils, rinsed and drained
4 cups water
3 large onions, chopped
1/2 cup salted butter
1 cup #3 bulgur wheat
1 tablespoon salt
1 (15 ounce) can black-eyed peas, drained

Method

In a saucepan, combine lentils and 3 cups of water. Bring to a boil and cook on medium until tender. Drain.

In another large pan, sauté onions in butter until light brown. Add 1 cup of water, wheat, salt, black-eyed peas and cooked lentils. Cover and simmer for 30 minutes or until liquid is absorbed and wheat is soft. Add more water if necessary.

For more flavor, substitute 1 cup of chicken broth for 1 cup of water.

Flavorful Bulgur Wheat Pilaf

Serves 6

Ingredients

4 teaspoons extra virgin olive oil
2 cups #2 or #3 bulgur wheat
4 cups chicken broth
Salt and pepper, to taste

Method

In a saucepan, heat olive oil and sauté wheat 8-10 minutes or until grains separate easily. Add salt and pepper.

Add chicken broth and bring to a boil. Cover tightly and simmer until all the liquid is absorbed and wheat is tender, approximately 20 minutes.

Serve with any Mediterranean dish instead of rice.

Bulgur Wheat Pilaf
with Butter

Serves 4

Ingredients

1/2 cup unsalted butter
1 cup #4 bulgur wheat
2 cups chicken broth
1 teaspoon salt

Method

In a saucepan, bring chicken broth to a boil. In a separate pan, melt butter. Add wheat and stir for 2 minutes over low heat. Pour boiling broth over the wheat and add salt.

Stir on low heat and cover for 20 minutes or until broth is absorbed.

Vegetables & Meatless

Colorful Roasted Vegetables

Serves 4-6

Ingredients

6 small red potatoes, unpeeled, quartered
1 small eggplant, peeled and cut into cubes
1 green bell pepper, cut into 1" pieces
1 yellow bell pepper, cut into 1" pieces
1 red bell pepper, cut into 1" pieces
1 small red onion, cut into chunks
4 carrots, peeled and cut into chunks
2 small yellow squash, cut into chunks
2 small zucchini, cut into chunks
5 cloves garlic, whole
1/2 teaspoon dried basil
1/2 teaspoon dried oregano
1/2 teaspoon dried chives
2 tablespoons extra virgin olive oil
2 tablespoons balsamic vinegar
Salt and pepper, to taste

Method

Pre-heat oven to 425°. In a small bowl, whisk together the oil, vinegar, herbs, garlic, salt and pepper. Place vegetables in a large shallow roasting pan. Drizzle wet ingredients over the vegetables. Stir to coat. Roast uncovered until vegetables are tender, stirring once during roasting time. Serve warm.

Greek Oven-Roasted Potatoes
with Feta Cheese

Serves 6

Ingredients

3 pounds red potatoes, unpeeled and cut into 1 1/2" cubes
1 large onion, cut in large chunks
4 cloves garlic, minced
3 tablespoons extra virgin olive oil
3/4 teaspoon kosher salt
3/4 teaspoon ground black pepper
1 tablespoon dried oregano
8 ounces feta cheese, room temperature

Method

Preheat oven to 450°. In a large bowl, combine all ingredients except cheese. Toss well.

Place potatoes in a single layer on an ungreased baking sheet. Bake for 1 hour, stirring occasionally, until potatoes are done. Transfer to a dish and crumble feta cheese on top. Toss until well blended.

Nahima's Parsleyed Potatoes

Serves 4

Ingredients

10 small red potatoes, unpeeled
1/4 cup extra virgin olive oil
1/2 cup fresh, flat-leaf parsley, minced or 2 tablespoons dried
Salt and pepper, to taste

Method

Scrub potatoes gently. Place in a saucepan and cover with water. Bring to a boil and cook until tender. Drain and cut into quarters. Add oil, salt, pepper and parsley. Toss until well coated.

Twice-Baked Greek Potatoes
with Feta Cheese

Serves 8

Ingredients

4 large baking potatoes
3 tablespoons salted butter, softened
1 (16 ounce) plain Greek yogurt
1/2 cup feta cheese, crumbled
2 tablespoons dried oregano
3 green onions, sliced
3/4 teaspoon kosher salt
1/2 teaspoon ground black pepper

Method

Pierce each potato 4 times with a fork. Place directly on oven rack. Bake at 450° for 1 hour or until tender. Let cool about 15 minutes.

Cut baked potatoes in half lengthwise. Be careful not to break or tear the skins. Scoop pulp into a large bowl, reserving potato shells. Add butter, yogurt, cheese, oregano, onions, salt and pepper. Mix well with a potato masher or fork. Spoon potato mixture evenly into reserved shells. Place stuffed shells on an ungreased baking sheet.

Bake at 450° for 25 minutes or until golden brown.

Simple Oven-Baked Potatoes
with Red Onions

Serves 4

Ingredients

2 large red onions, thinly sliced into rings
3 russet potatoes, unpeeled, sliced
1 1/2 cup salted butter, melted
8 tablespoons Parmesan cheese, grated
Salt and pepper, to taste

Method

Dip potato slices and onion rings into butter to coat. Arrange on a shallow baking sheet. Sprinkle both sides with grated Parmesan cheese, salt, and pepper.

Bake at 350° for 30 minutes or until fork tender.

Teanne Vegetarian Grape Leaves

Serves 6-8

Ingredients

1 (16 ounce) jar grape leaves, drained
1 (15 ounce) can chickpeas, drained, coarsely chopped
1 cup extra virgin olive oil
2 cloves garlic, minced
1 cup parboiled, long-grain white rice, uncooked,
   washed and drained
3 bunches fresh, flat-leaf parsley leaves, chopped
1 large white onion, finely chopped
1 bunch green onions, finely chopped
4 large tomatoes, diced
1/2 cup lemon juice
Salt and pepper, to taste

Method

In a bowl, combine chickpeas, garlic, onions, tomatoes, parsley, oil, rice, salt and pepper. Mix well.

Lay grape leaves on a plate smooth side down; cut stems. Place leaves one at a time on a flat surface; spread 1 teaspoon of mixture in center of leaf near stem. Fold sides in, over filling, and roll leaf very tightly. Repeat method until all leaves are rolled. Left-over leaves can be used to line the bottom of your pan.

Line rolled grape leaves in the pan side by side. Cover the bottom. Place second row of leaves in the opposite direction. Continue until all rolled leaves are in the pot.

Cover with a heavy plate to keep them in place while cooking. Add water to cover the top of the plate. Bring to a boil. Cover and simmer for 40-45 minutes until rice is done.

Remove plate. Pour lemon juice over leaves. Cool completely. Remove leaves gently to avoid breakage.

Can be served hot or cold.

Riesling off-dry or
Vinho Verde

Stewed Squash and Zucchini
with Chickpeas

Serves 4

Ingredients

1 tablespoon extra virgin olive oil
1 cup chicken broth
1/2 teaspoon cayenne pepper
1 teaspoon ground cumin
1 teaspoon ground cinnamon
1 large zucchini, cut into cubes
1 large yellow squash, cut into cubes
1 (16 ounce) can chickpeas, drained
1 (14.5 ounce) can diced tomatoes, undrained
3 tablespoons fresh, flat-leaf parsley, chopped

Method

In a large skillet, heat oil over medium-high heat. Add zucchini
and yellow squash. Cook on medium-low heat until brown.
Add chickpeas, tomatoes, seasonings and chicken broth. Bring
to a boil; then simmer on low, uncovered, until tender. Garnish
with chopped parsley.

Sancerre

Zucchini and Pine Nut Sauté

Serves 4

Ingredients

1 pound zucchini, sliced
1 small onion, chopped
2 cloves garlic, minced
1 cup fresh mushrooms, sliced
1 tablespoon pine nuts
2 tablespoons extra virgin olive oil
1 teaspoon salt
1/2 teaspoon ground black pepper
1/2 teaspoon dried thyme
1/2 cup Parmesan cheese, grated

Method

In a saucepan, sauté onions, garlic and pine nuts in olive oil. When tender and light brown, add remaining ingredients except cheese.

Cook on low heat, stirring often for 10 minutes, or until zucchini is crisp-tender. Sprinkle with cheese.

Summer Squash
with Tomatoes

Serves 6

Ingredients

2 pounds yellow squash
3 ripe tomatoes, finely chopped
1/3 cup extra virgin olive oil
1 large onion, chopped
3/4 cup chicken broth
1 teaspoon salt
1/2 teaspoon ground black pepper
1/2 teaspoon allspice

Method

Wash squash and pat dry. Cut into 1 1/2" cubes. In a large skillet, brown onions until tender. Add squash and sauté for 10 minutes. Add tomatoes and chicken broth. Sprinkle with salt, pepper and allspice.

Cook uncovered on medium heat for 30 minutes until tender.

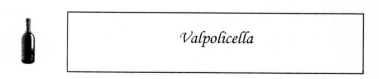

Valpolicella

Spicy Eggplant Tortellini

Serves 4

Ingredients

1 large eggplant, peeled and chopped
1 medium onion, cut into thin wedges
1 (28 ounce) can diced tomatoes, undrained
3 tablespoons garlic, finely chopped
1/4 cup extra virgin olive oil
1 tablespoon Italian seasoning
1 teaspoon dried basil
1/2 teaspoon red pepper flakes
1/4 cup Parmesan cheese, grated
1 (9 ounce) package fresh or frozen tortellini

Method

In a large skillet, heat oil over medium-high heat. Cook and stir eggplant and onion for 15 minutes. Stir in tomatoes, garlic, Italian seasoning, basil and red pepper flakes. Reduce heat, cover and simmer 15 minutes or until tender.

Cook tortellini as directed on package; drain. Place in a large serving bowl. Combine tortellini and eggplant mixture. Toss gently. Sprinkle with grated Parmesan cheese.

Nahima's Spinach Pies

Serves 14

Ingredients

14 frozen dinner rolls, thawed according to package
2 (10 ounce) packages frozen chopped spinach
1 large onion, diced
2 tablespoons pine nuts
3/4 cup lemon juice
1 1/2 teaspoons salt
1 teaspoon ground black pepper
1/8 cup extra virgin olive oil

Method

Defrost spinach in refrigerator. Squeeze out water.

In a saucepan, sauté onions and pine nuts in olive oil until light brown. Add salt and pepper.

Place spinach in a mixing bowl. Add lemon juice, pine nuts and onions. Mix together.

Flatten defrosted rolls as directed on package to about 4" in diameter. Place 2 tablespoons of spinach mixture in the center of each roll. Fold over 3 sides to form a triangle and pinch together to seal. Make sure all the filling stays inside.

Lightly grease a baking sheet with olive oil. Place pies on baking sheet about 1/2 inch apart. Let rise for 30 minutes. Bake at 400° for 25 minutes or until light brown.

Spinach and Feta Cheese Pies

Serves 14

Ingredients

14 frozen dinner rolls, thawed according to package
2 (10 ounce) packages frozen chopped spinach
1 (8 ounce) package feta cheese, crumbled
1 large onion, diced
2 tablespoons pine nuts
3/4 cup lemon juice
1 1/2 teaspoons salt
1 teaspoon ground black pepper
1/8 cup extra virgin olive oil

Method

Defrost spinach in refrigerator. Squeeze out water.

In a saucepan, sauté onions and pine nuts in olive oil until light brown. Add salt and pepper.

Place spinach in a mixing bowl. Add feta cheese, lemon juice, pine nuts and onions. Mix together.

Flatten defrosted rolls as directed on package to about 4" in diameter. Place 2 tablespoons of spinach mixture in the center of each roll. Fold over 3 sides to form a triangle and pinch together to seal. Make sure all the filling stays inside.

Lightly grease a baking sheet with olive oil. Place pies on baking sheet about 1/2 inch apart. Let rise for 30 minutes. Bake at 400° for 25 minutes or until light brown.

Roasted Herbed Vegetables
with Pine Nuts

Serves 8

Ingredients

12 small red potatoes, unpeeled, quartered
2 carrots, peeled and cut into 1" pieces
2 stalks of celery, cut into 2" pieces
1 medium red onion, quartered
4 cloves garlic, sliced
2 tablespoons pine nuts
4 tablespoons extra virgin olive oil
1/2 teaspoon dried thyme
1/2 teaspoon dried sage
1/2 teaspoon dried rosemary

Method

Pre-heat oven to 450°. In a large bowl, combine all ingredients. Stir until well blended. Layer vegetables in a single layer on an ungreased baking sheet. Bake for about 45 minutes or until vegetables are tender.

Pine Nut Vegetable Sauté

Serves 2-4

Ingredients

1 large onion, chopped
1 medium green bell pepper, chopped
2 cloves garlic, minced
8 ounces fresh mushrooms, sliced
3 stalks celery, chopped
3 tablespoons extra virgin olive oil
1/4 cup pine nuts
Salt and pepper, to taste

Method

In a saucepan, sauté onions, celery and garlic until tender. Stir in pine nuts and sauté until light brown. Add mushroom and cook on medium-low heat until done. Add salt and pepper.

Serve with any meat or rice dish.

Meatless Stuffed Yellow Squash

Ingredients

24 small yellow squash
1 1/2 cups parboiled, long-grain white rice, uncooked
1/2 cup pine nuts
1 bunch green onions, finely chopped
4 cloves garlic, minced
1 (6 ounce) can tomato paste
1 (14.5 ounce) can tomato sauce
Salt and pepper, to taste

Method

Cut neck off of squash and core out with a vegetable corer. Be careful not to puncture. Wash squash well with water and drain upside down on a paper towel.

In a bowl, combine remaining ingredients, except tomato sauce. Stuff squash 3/4 full and place neck up in a saucepan. Pour tomato sauce over squash. Put a plate on top. Add water until squash is covered. Bring to a boil. Cover and cook on low heat for 45 minutes.

Riesling
(preferably dry)

Perfect Pasta
with Feta Cheese and Sun-dried Tomatoes

Serves 4

Ingredients

1 small onion, chopped
1 small red bell pepper, chopped
1 small green bell pepper, chopped
4 cloves garlic, minced
4 ounces feta cheese, crumbled
2 tablespoons sun-dried tomatoes, chopped
1 1/2 teaspoon Italian seasoning
1/4 teaspoon dried basil or 1 teaspoon fresh, chopped
4 tablespoons extra virgin olive oil
1 (8 ounce) package pasta of choice
Cooking sherry, to taste
Flat-leaf parsley, to taste

Method

In a saucepan, sauté onion, peppers, garlic and tomatoes in oil.
Stir in Italian seasoning, basil, parsley and sherry. Simmer
while pasta is cooking. Cook pasta according to package
directions; drain.

In a large serving bowl, combine cooked pasta and sauce; toss
well. Top with feta cheese and fresh parsley

Chardonnay
(preferably unoaked)

Easy Chickpea Wrap

Serves 4-6

Ingredients

1 (15 ounce) can chickpeas, drained and rinsed
1/2 cup sour cream
1 teaspoon lemon juice
1/2 teaspoon garlic, minced
8 flour tortillas, white or wheat
1 cup mozzarella cheese, grated
Salt and pepper, to taste

Method

In a food processor, combine chickpeas, sour cream, lemon juice, and seasonings. Spread mixture on tortillas, dividing equally. Roll tortillas and place on an ungreased baking sheet. Sprinkle with cheese. Bake at 350° for 8-10 minutes until cheese is melted.

Vegetarian Pita Pockets
with Feta Cheese

Serves 4

Ingredients

1 (15 ounce) can chickpeas, drained and rinsed
2 cups shredded romaine lettuce
2 green onions, thinly sliced
1/2 cup celery, chopped
1/2 cup red bell pepper, chopped,
1/2 cup feta cheese, crumbled
1/4 cup kalamata olives, chopped
1/2 cup Mediterranean Basic Salad Dressing
   (see recipe page 50)
4 (6 inch) pita bread rounds

Method

In a large bowl, combine all ingredients except lettuce and pita bread. Toss gently; cover and chill overnight.

Cut pita bread in half; spoon mixture into the bread and lettuce and serve.

Easy Pickled Cucumbers and Onions

Ingredients

3 English cucumbers, unpeeled, thinly sliced
1 large sweet onion, thinly sliced
3/4 cup sugar
1/2 cup white vinegar
1/2 cup water
Salt and pepper, to taste

Method

In a bowl, mix all ingredients together. Place in clean jars. Cover and chill 2-3 hours in refrigerator.

Middle Eastern Pickled Turnips
(Umhalla/Lifet)

Serves 10

Ingredients

10 small turnips, unpeeled
1 cup white vinegar
1 clove garlic, whole
2 cups water
2 teaspoons salt

Method

Wash turnips and cut into cubes. Place in a jar and add remaining ingredients. Cover with lid and shake. Let stand at room temperature for 3 days, then refrigerate.

Can be used as a garnish or on a relish tray.

Pickled Cauliflower and Carrots

Ingredients

1 medium sized head of cauliflower
4 carrots, peeled
2 cups water
1 cup white vinegar
2 teaspoons salt
1 (15 ounce) can beets (use only juice)

Method

Wash carrots and dice into rounds. Wash cauliflower and separate into flowerets. Place in pan with enough water to cover and boil until partially tender.

Mix water, vinegar and salt together. Pack the carrots and cauliflower into clean jars. Cover with vinegar solution. Add the beet juice until vegetables are completely covered. Cover with lid and shake gently.

Allow to stand 3 days at room temperature, then refrigerate until ready to serve.

Can be used as a garnish or on a relish tray.

Beef & Pork

Nahima's Open Face Meat Pies
(Sfeeha)

Yield 50 pies

Ingredients

1 pound ground sirloin or ground chuck
1/4 cup pine nuts
1/2 teaspoon ground black pepper
1 teaspoon salt
1 large onion, finely chopped
3 tablespoons salted butter
50 frozen dinner rolls

Method

In a skillet, sauté onions. Add beef to onions and brown. Add pine nuts, salt and pepper. Stir until well mixed. Drain oil.

Thaw rolls and let rise as directed on package. Place rolls on an ungreased baking sheet. Flatten with hand to make a circle. Place 1 tablespoon of meat mixture on top of roll and spread evenly. Bake at 400° for 25 minutes or until brown. Serve warm.

Aromatic Arabian Rice
with Ground Meat

Serves 6-8

Ingredients

1 pound ground chuck, turkey or lamb
1/2 cup pine nuts
1 cup long-grain white rice, uncooked
2 cups water
1 teaspoon salt
1/2 teaspoon ground black pepper
1/2 teaspoon ground cinnamon
1 tablespoon salted butter

Method

In a saucepan, bring water to a boil. Add salt, butter and rice.
Cover and simmer 15-20 minutes until tender.

In a skillet, sauté the ground meat and pine nuts. When cooked
through, add seasonings and stir well.

Combine meat mixture with cooked rice. Toss well and serve
hot.

Contemporary Stuffed Yellow Squash Boats
With Ground Sirloin

Serves 6-8 or more

Ingredients

1 pound ground sirloin
8 medium yellow squash
4 cloves garlic, minced
2 large onions, finely chopped
1/2 teaspoon salt
1/4 teaspoon ground black pepper
3 tablespoons extra virgin olive oil
1 (14.5 ounce) can tomato sauce

Method

In a medium saucepan, sauté garlic and onions in olive oil until tender. Add beef and sauté until brown.

Clean squash. Cut off tops and slice lengthwise. Gently remove inside of squash being careful not to tear the flesh. Place in a 3" deep roaster pan. Fill each squash with meat mixture. Press firmly. Pour tomato sauce over top. Bake at 350° until squash is tender, about 35 minutes.

Gamay

Nahima's Stuffed Yellow Squash
With Meat and Rice
(Kousa-mihshi)

Serves 15 or more

Ingredients

3 pounds ground chuck or sirloin
15 – 20 medium size yellow squash
1 1/2 to 2 cups parboiled, long-grain white rice, uncooked
1 (6 ounce) can tomato paste
1 (14.5 ounce) can tomato sauce
6 cloves garlic, minced
2 teaspoons salt
1/2 teaspoon ground black pepper

Method

Cut neck off of squash and core out with a vegetable corer, being careful not to puncture. Wash squash well and drain upside down on a paper towel.

Combine rice, meat, tomato paste, salt, pepper, and garlic in a bowl. Mix well. Stuff squash with rice and meat mixture. Do not pack too tightly. You want to allow space for the rice to swell. Place squash filling side up in a large pot. Arrange standing straight up. Pour tomato sauce over squash and put a plate on top to secure squash in place. Add water to cover the top of the squash. Bring to a boil, then reduce heat, simmer on low for 45 minutes or until rice is cooked. Take out gently and serve on a platter.

Nahima's Stuffed Bell Peppers
with Meat and Rice

Serves 10

Ingredients

2 pounds ground chuck or sirloin
10 small to medium green bell peppers
1 to 1 1/2 cups parboiled, long-grain white rice, uncooked
1 (6 ounce) can tomato paste
1 (14.5 ounce) can tomato sauce
5 cloves garlic, minced
2 teaspoons salt
1/2 teaspoon ground black pepper

Method

Wash peppers. Cut off top and hollow out the center. Rinse and drain upside down on a paper towel.

In a bowl, combine rice, meat, tomato paste, salt, pepper and garlic. Mix well. Stuff pepper with rice and meat mixture. Do not pack too tightly.

Place peppers filling side up in a large pot. Pour tomato sauce over the peppers and put a plate on top to secure in place. Add water to cover the top of the peppers.

Bring to a boil, then reduce heat to low. Simmer for 45 minutes or until rice is cooked. Remove from pan gently and serve on a platter.

Nahima's Stuffed Rolled Green Cabbage Leaves
(Yabra-mal-foot)

Serves 10 or more

Ingredients

1 pound ground chuck
1 large head of green cabbage (lighter color is more tender)
3/4 cup parboiled, long-grain white rice, uncooked
1 teaspoon salt
1/4 teaspoon ground black pepper
1 (6 ounce) can tomato paste
1 (15 ounce) can tomato sauce
6 cloves garlic, minced

Method

Cut core from center of the cabbage. Place in a large pot of boiling water. As the leaves become limp, pull each leaf off the head of cabbage. Set aside until all leaves are completely separated. Cut the hard center from each leaf. Cut large leaves in half. Tough or small leaves can be used to layer the bottom of the pot.

Mix remaining ingredients in a bowl. Place one leaf, smooth side down, on a flat surface. Place 1 tablespoon of meat mixture in the center of the cabbage leaf. Spread evenly. Roll tightly without tucking in sides. Continue with each leaf until all are rolled.

Place remaining leaves in the bottom of a large pot. Arrange stuffed leaves side by side to cover the bottom. Then start another row placing them in the opposite direction.

When finished, pour tomato sauce over the leaves. Add a heavy plate on top to secure leaves in place. Fill pot with water to cover the top of the leaves.

Bring to a gentle boil, careful not to break the leaves. Cover, reduce heat and simmer on medium-low heat for 45 minutes. Remove gently and serve on a platter.

Riesling or Gewurztraminer
(preferably Alsatian)

Nahima's Traditional Rolled Grape Leaves
(Whadda Adeesh)

Serves 10 or more

Ingredients

1 1/2 pounds ground sirloin or chuck
1 (16 ounce) jar grape leaves, drained
1 (6 ounce) can tomato paste
10 cloves garlic, minced
1 cup parboiled, long-grain white rice, uncooked,
    washed and drained
1 teaspoon salt
1 teaspoon ground black pepper
1 cup lemon juice
4 large tomatoes, finely diced

Method

In a large bowl, combine meat, rice, garlic, salt, pepper, tomatoes and tomato paste. Mix well.

Lay grape leaves on a plate smooth side down; cut stems. Place leaves one at a time on a flat surface. Spread with 1 tablespoon of mixture. Fold sides in and roll leaf very tightly. Repeat method until all leaves are rolled.

Left-over leaves can be used to line the bottom of the pan. Line rolled grape leaves in large pot side by side. Cover the bottom.

Place second row in the opposite direction. Cover with a heavy plate to keep them in place while cooking. Add water to cover the plate.

Bring to a boil. Cover and simmer for 40-45 minutes until rice is done. Remove plate.

Pour lemon juice over leaves while hot. Cool 5-10 minutes, then remove leaves gently to avoid breakage. Place on platter and garnish with sliced lemons.

Contemporary method - Use chicken broth instead of water for extra flavor.

Arneis

Stuffed Eggplant
with Meat and Pine Nuts

Serves 2

Ingredients

1/2 pound ground chuck
1 medium eggplant
1 onion, finely chopped
1 large tomato, diced
1 clove garlic, minced
1/2 cup Italian bread crumbs
1/2 cup Parmesan cheese, grated
2 tablespoons salted butter
2 tablespoons pine nuts

Method

Remove top of eggplant and cut in half, lengthwise. Scoop out the pulp.

In a saucepan, bring water to a boil. Parboil the eggplant shells by dropping them into the boiling water for 5 minutes. Remove from water and drain on a paper towel.

Place drained eggplant in a greased baking dish.

In a saucepan, sauté beef, onions, garlic, pine nuts, and bell pepper in butter until brown. Add tomatoes, salt and pepper. Simmer for 20 minutes until well done. Stir in bread crumbs.

Stuff eggplant shells with mixture and top with cheese. Bake at 350° for 30 minutes.

Stuffed Tender Tomatoes
with Meat and Pine Nuts

Serves 4-6

Ingredients

1 pound ground chuck
6 large firm tomatoes
1/2 cup pine nuts
2 medium onions, finely chopped
2 cloves garlic, minced
1 teaspoon salt
1/2 teaspoon ground black pepper
1 tablespoon tomato paste
4 tablespoons extra virgin olive oil

Method

Wash tomatoes. Slice off top and gently scoop out the pulp. Save the tops.

In a saucepan, sauté onions and garlic in olive oil until light brown. Add pine nuts and brown for a couple of minutes. Add beef and brown until no longer pink. Drain. Add tomato paste, salt and pepper. Mix well.

Fill tomatoes with meat mixture and replace tops. Arrange on an ungreased baking dish close together. Bake uncovered at 350° for 30 minutes or until tomatoes are tender.

> Barbera, Chianti or Sangiovese
> (preferably from Italy)

Stuffed Potatoes
with Beef and Pine Nuts

Serves 4-6

Ingredients

2 pounds ground sirloin
4 pounds medium baking potatoes
1/2 cup salted butter
2 cloves garlic, minced
2 large onions, finely chopped
1 teaspoon salt
1/2 teaspoon ground black pepper
1/2 cup pine nuts
1 (6 ounce) can tomato paste
2 tablespoons lemon juice

Method

Peel and hollow out potatoes with a vegetable corer. In a large skillet, brown potatoes in butter. Remove from pan and set aside.

In the same skillet, sauté meat, onions, garlic and pine nuts. Add remaining ingredients and mix well.

Stuff potatoes tightly. Arrange in a large pot, standing up with open end on top. Put a plate on top and add water to cover potatoes. Bring to a boil. Reduce heat and simmer for 1 hour.

Nahima's Ground Meat
with Wheat
(Kibbi Nayye) Raw

Serves 4-6

Ingredients

2 pounds very lean ground sirloin (ground twice)
2 1/2 cups fine #1 cracked bulgur wheat
2 tablespoons salt
1 teaspoon ground black pepper
1 large onion, quartered
2 cups water with ice cubes

Method

Have butcher grind top sirloin twice per order (not pre-packaged)

Cover wheat with cold water in a bowl. Let soak 20 minutes. Drain excess water. Add meat to wheat, salt and pepper. Mix with hands, kneading and adding small amounts of ice water to give a thick consistency.

When mixed well, put on a platter. Flatten out into a round mound. Place onions around kibbi. Chill in refrigerator until ready to serve.

(Consuming raw or undercooked meat may increase your risk of food borne illness.)

Nahima's Baked Meat and Wheat
(Kibbi Sanee)

Serves 8-10

Make Nahima's Ground Meat with Wheat (Raw Kibbi)
 (see recipe page 129)
Make Pine Nut and Meat Filling for kibbi (Hashwa)
 (see recipe page 131)

Ingredients

1 cup salted butter, melted

Method

Grease a 13 x 9 x 2 or 10 x 14 baking pan. Make several balls and pat them flat, then layer raw kibbi on the bottom, using about half of the mixture or balls. Dip hands in water as you apply to make smooth. Spread all of the pine nut and meat filling on top as a second layer. Add the remaining raw kibbi on top as a third layer. Spread evenly. Score in squares or triangles with a knife.

Loosen edges from tray with a spatula. Pour 1 cup of melted butter over top. Bake at 350° for 45 minutes or until golden brown. Broil for a few minutes if necessary until the top is golden brown.

Nahima's Pine Nuts and Meat Filling
(Hashwah)

Ingredients

1 pound ground sirloin
2 medium onions, finely chopped
1/2 cup salted butter
1/2 cup pine nuts
1/3 teaspoon ground black pepper
1 teaspoon salt, or to taste
1/2 cup water

Method

In a saucepan, sauté onions and pine nuts in butter on low until done. Add beef, stirring occasionally. When meat is cooked, add water and stir until absorbed.

Suggested use:

Pita Pockets with Pine Nuts and Meat Filling

Place mixture inside half a pocket of pita bread. Serving size depends on how much filling you add to each pocket.

Nahima's Fried Kibbi Balls

Yield 15 – 20 balls

Make Nahima's Ground Meat with Wheat
  (See recipe page 129)
Make Pine Nuts and Meat Filling recipe
  (See recipe page 131)

Ingredients

Canola oil to fry

Method

Roll raw kibbi into golf ball sized-balls. Make a hole inside each ball by pressing one finger through center of ball.

Stuff each ball with about 2 teaspoons of meat and nut filling. Gently close the opening with wet fingers and smooth out into balls or an oval shape.

In a skillet, fry each ball individually in canola oil, turning until golden brown. Place on a paper towel to drain excess oil.

Nahima's Syrian Dish
with Meat and Bulgur Wheat
(Bid-dfin)

Serves 6

Ingredients

Your choice of:
   1 slab pork ribs, trimmed and cut into pieces
   2 pounds skinless, boneless chicken breasts, cut into pieces
   2 pounds sirloin, cut into pieces
1/2 cup salted butter
2 cups #3 bulgur wheat
3 cups water or chicken broth
Salt, to taste

Method

In a large pot, brown meat in butter on all sides on medium heat. Cover, reduce heat to low and simmer until meat is tender, about 1 1/2 hours. Add bulgur to cooked meat. Add liquid to reach the top of the bulgur. Add salt. Cover and cook on low until bulgur is done. Serve with sweet onions.

Lebanese Green Beans and Beef
(Yuknee Lubee)

Serves 4

Ingredients

1 pound sirloin, cut in cubes
1 pound fresh green beans, trimmed and snapped
1 tablespoon salted butter
1 medium onion, chopped
2 cloves garlic, chopped
1 (15 ounce) can diced tomatoes, undrained
1/4 teaspoon ground black pepper
1 teaspoon salt

Method

In a saucepan, sauté meat in butter until light brown. Add onions and garlic and cook until onions are tender. Place beans over meat; add salt, pepper and tomatoes. Bring to a boil. Reduce heat, cover and simmer until meat is tender.

Serve with any rice or grain.

Exciting Eggplant Casserole
with Ground Meat

Serves 4

Ingredients

1 pound ground chuck, beef or sirloin
1 medium eggplant, unpeeled
1/2 onion, chopped
1/2 green bell pepper, chopped
2-3 cloves garlic, minced
1 (14.5 ounce) can diced tomatoes, undrained
1 tablespoon all-purpose flour
1/4 teaspoon ground black pepper
1 cup sharp cheddar cheese, grated
1/4 teaspoon dried oregano
2 tablespoons pine nuts
Salt and pepper, to taste

Method

Slice eggplant about 1/4 inch thick. In a pan, cover eggplant with water and boil for 3-5 minutes until tender. Drain.

In a skillet, sauté meat, onions, garlic, bell pepper, oregano, salt and pepper. Cook until tender. Add flour and stir well. Add tomatoes and continue to cook on medium heat for about 5 minutes.

In a casserole dish, arrange in layers; 1/2 eggplant, 1/2 meat, 1/2 cheese, repeat. Top with pine nuts. Bake uncovered at 350° for 25 minutes.

Quick Bulgur Wheat and Ground Meat

Serves 6

Ingredients

1 pound ground chuck or ground turkey
3/4 cup #3 bulgur wheat, soaked and drained
2/3 cup diced onions
1/2 cup green bell pepper, chopped
1 teaspoon salt
1 teaspoon chili powder
1 clove garlic, minced
1/8 teaspoon ground black pepper
2 tablespoons extra virgin olive oil

Method

In a skillet, brown meat until done. Drain fat. Stir in remaining ingredients and simmer for 10-15 minutes, uncovered.

Serve with a vegetable of choice.

Scrambled Eggs with Ground Meat

Serves 2

Ingredients

3/4 cups ground sirloin beef or ground turkey
2 tablespoons salted butter
2 eggs, beaten
1/2 teaspoon salt
1/8 teaspoon ground black pepper
1/2 cup chopped onions

Method

In a skillet, melt butter. Add onions and sauté until clear. Add ground meat and cook until brown. Add beaten eggs, salt and pepper. Continue stirring until eggs are done.

Can also add fresh chopped mushrooms.

Marinated Beef Kabobs

Serves 12

Ingredients

3 pounds sirloin tip beef
1/2 cup lemon juice
1/4 cup Worcestershire sauce
1 cup extra virgin olive oil
3/4 cup soy sauce
1/4 cup prepared yellow mustard or Dijon mustard
2 garlic cloves, pressed
2 large green bell peppers, cut into cubes
1/2 pound fresh mushroom caps
12 cherry tomatoes
12 pearl onions

Method

Trim fat from beef and cut into 1 1/2 inch cubes. Combine lemon juice, Worcestershire sauce, olive oil, soy sauce, mustard and garlic in a bowl. Mix well. Add meat and cover with plastic wrap. Refrigerate for 12 hours, turning meat occasionally. Remove meat from marinade, reserving marinade. If using wooden skewers, soak them in water for 15 minutes. Alternate meat and vegetables. Cook inside on a grill pan or outside on a grill. Baste all with leftover marinade occasionally. Grill 15 minutes or until desired doneness.

*Instead of using skewers, you can use a long stem of rosemary. Pull off leaves, except a few on top. Thread ingredients onto the stem.

Grilled Arabic Meat on a Stick
(Kafta)

Serves 4-6

Ingredients

1 pound ground round steak
1 tablespoon zattar seasoning
2 tablespoons dried parsley
1 tablespoon dried mint
2 tablespoons dried marjoram
1 teaspoon salt
1/2 teaspoon paprika
1 small onion, minced
1 clove garlic, minced

Method

In a bowl, mix all ingredients together. Chill in refrigerator for 1 hour. Form chilled meat into individual balls the size of an egg. Mold and thread onto a metal or wooden skewers. Soak skewers in water for 15 minutes. Put 2-3 balls per skewer.

Grill inside on grill pan, in oven, or outside, turning occasionally until done.

St. Laurent

139

Grilled Lebanese Meat on a Stick
(Kafta)

Serves 4-6

Ingredients

1 pound fine ground round steak (have butcher grind twice)
1/2 teaspoon dried coriander
4 tablespoons dried parsley
2 tablespoons dried mint
2 tablespoons dried marjoram
1 teaspoon salt
1/2 teaspoon paprika
1/2 teaspoon ground cumin
1 medium onion, minced

Method

In a bowl, mix all ingredients together. Chill in refrigerator for 1 hour. Form chilled meat into individual balls the size of an egg. Mold and thread onto metal or wooden skewers. Soak skewers in water for 15 minutes. Put 2-3 balls per skewer.

Grill inside on grill pan, in oven, or outside, turning occasionally until done

Flipped Pork and Rice
(Riz-bi-dfeen)

Serves 4-6

Ingredients

3 pounds boneless center cut pork chops cut in small cubes
1 cup long-grain white rice, uncooked, washed and drained
3 medium onions, chopped
2 cloves garlic, chopped
1 (15 ounce) can chickpeas, drained
4 tablespoons salted butter
2 cups chicken broth

Method

In a medium pot, melt butter and sauté onions and garlic until tender. Add pork and cook thoroughly.

In another medium pot, combine chickpeas and chicken broth. Bring to a boil, then add rice, garlic, onions, and pork. Reduce heat to low, cook for 30-45 minutes until all the liquid is absorbed and rice is tender. Let stand in pot for 15 minutes.

Put a platter on top of pot, then flip the ingredients onto the platter. You should see layered chickpeas, rice and pork.

Nahima's Green Beans and Pork Spare Ribs
(Loubieh)

Serves 4-6

Ingredients

1 slab pork spare ribs
3 pounds fresh string beans
8-10 small red potatoes, whole
2 large onions, chopped
1 (31 ounce) can diced tomatoes, undrained
2 tablespoons extra virgin olive oil
1 cup chicken broth
2 tablespoons salted butter
Salt and pepper, to taste

Method

Wash and snap green beans. Trim fat from spare ribs and cut into pieces. Scrape a little flesh off of red potatoes.

In a large pot, sauté ribs in oil and butter until brown. Add onions and simmer on low until fork tender. Add green beans, tomatoes, salt, pepper and broth.

When beans are almost done, add potatoes. Continue cooking until potatoes are tender.

Chicken

Juicy Chickpea Chicken
with Spices

Serves 6

Ingredients

6 boneless, skinless chicken breasts
2/3 cup orange juice
1 teaspoon ground cinnamon
1/4 teaspoon curry powder
1/8 teaspoon allspice
1/8 teaspoon salt
1/8 teaspoon ground black pepper
1 (15 ounce) can chickpeas, drained
1 teaspoon honey

Method

In a bowl, whisk together orange juice, honey, cinnamon, curry powder and allspice. Salt and pepper both sides of chicken. Place chicken in a baking dish. Pour orange juice mixture over chicken. Add chickpeas. Bake at 350° for 1 hour.

Apricot Baked Chicken
with Dijon Mustard

Serves 4

Ingredients

4 boneless, skinless chicken breasts
1/2 cup orange juice
12 dried apricots
1/2 cup brown sugar
1 tablespoon Dijon mustard
1 teaspoon allspice
1/2 teaspoon salt (optional)
1/2 teaspoon garlic powder

Method

In a saucepan combine orange juice, apricots, brown sugar, mustard, and allspice. Bring to a boil. Reduce heat and simmer on low until sugar is dissolved. Set aside.

Sprinkle chicken breasts with salt and garlic powder. Place chicken in a baking dish. Pour orange juice mixture over chicken. Bake uncovered at 350° for 1 hour, basting occasionally.

> Riesling
> (preferably Kabinett from Germany)

Nahima's Baked Chicken
with Lemon and Garlic

Serves 6

Ingredients

3 to 3 1/2 pounds cut-up chicken
4 tablespoons extra virgin olive oil
1/4 cup lemon juice
3 cloves garlic, minced
Salt and pepper, to taste

Method

In a bowl, mix together oil, juice and garlic. Salt and pepper chicken on all sides. Place chicken in a roaster pan. Pour oil mixture over the chicken.

Place in oven on broil until chicken is brown on both sides. Turn oven to 350° and continue to bake, uncovered, until juices run clear.

> *Champagne or Sauvignon Blanc
> (preferably from California)
> or Riesling (preferably off-dry German)*

Baked Kalamata Olive Chicken

Serves 4

Ingredients

4 boneless, skinless chicken breasts,
3 large white potatoes, peeled and cut in chunks
3 large carrots cut in 1/4" thick rounds
1/2 cup salted butter, melted
4 tablespoons lemon juice
2 cloves garlic, chopped
1/4 cup white wine
1/2 teaspoon salt
1/2 tablespoon dried oregano
1/2 teaspoon ground black pepper
8 kalamata olives, pitted and chopped
2 tablespoons olive juice (from the jar)

Method

Place chicken, potatoes and carrots in a 9 x 13 inch baking dish. Combine other ingredients, mix well and pour over chicken. Bake uncovered at 350° for 45 minutes to 1 hour, basting occasionally.

Basil Pesto Chicken

Serves 4

Ingredients

4 boneless, skinless chicken breasts
2 cups fresh basil
2 tablespoons pine nuts
2 cloves garlic, minced
1 teaspoon salt
1/2 cup extra virgin olive oil
1/2 cup Parmesan cheese, grated
2 tablespoons Romano cheese, grated

Method

In a food processor or blender, combine basil, pine nuts, garlic and salt. Slowly add olive oil. Blend on high speed, scraping sides occasionally. Pour into a bowl and add both cheeses. Mix with a spoon or spatula to blend.

Place chicken in a baking dish. Pour pesto mixture over chicken. Bake uncovered at 350° for 1 hour.

Chablis, Vermentino
or Unoaked Chardonnay
(preferably from Italy)

Nahima's Chicken
with Fresh Vegetables

Serves 4

Ingredients

4 boneless, skinless chicken breasts
3/4 cup onion, chopped
3/4 cup green bell pepper, chopped
3/4 cup red bell pepper, chopped
1 cup fresh tomatoes, diced
3/4 cup zucchini, chopped
3/4 cup yellow squash, chopped
2 tablespoons extra virgin olive oil
1/4 teaspoon dried basil
1/8 teaspoon ground black pepper
1/4 teaspoon dried rosemary
3 cloves garlic, chopped
1/4 cup dry white wine

Method

In a large skillet, heat oil. Add garlic and onions. Cook on low heat until tender. Add chicken. Brown on both sides.

Add remaining ingredients. Mix well. Cover and simmer until chicken and vegetables are done.

Delicious Dijon Chicken
with Capers

Serves 8

Ingredients

8 boneless, skinless chicken breasts
2 tablespoons capers
1/4 cup salted butter or extra virgin olive oil
1/4 cup lemon juice
2 tablespoons Worcestershire sauce
1 tablespoon Dijon mustard
1/4 cup fresh chives, chopped
1/4 cup fresh, flat-leaf parsley, chopped

Method

In a large skillet, sauté the chicken in butter or olive oil over medium heat until done. Stir in lemon juice, Worcestershire sauce, mustard and capers until well blended. Simmer on low heat for 5 minutes. Garnish with parsley and chives.

Sauvignon Blanc
(preferably from New Zealand)

Dijon Mustard Chicken
with Pine Nuts

Serves 4

Ingredients

4 boneless, skinless chicken breasts
2 tablespoons Dijon mustard
1 tablespoon lime juice
1/8 teaspoon ground black pepper
1/8 teaspoon salt
1 teaspoon ground cumin
2 tablespoons pine nuts, toasted

Method

In a bowl, whisk together mustard, lime juice, and cumin. Salt and pepper both sides of chicken. Place chicken in a baking dish. Pour mustard mixture over chicken. Bake uncovered at 350° for 1 hour. Sprinkle toasted pine nuts over chicken before serving.

Easy Baked Chicken
with Herbs

Serves 6

Ingredients

6 boneless, skinless chicken breasts
2 tablespoons extra virgin olive oil
2 cloves garlic, minced
2 teaspoons paprika
2 teaspoons dried rosemary
1 teaspoon dried thyme
1 teaspoon dried parsley flakes
1 teaspoon dried tarragon
1 teaspoon dried oregano
1/8 teaspoon salt
1/8 teaspoon ground black pepper

Method

Rub chicken with olive oil and garlic. In a bowl, mix together herbs, salt, pepper and paprika. Sprinkle over each piece of chicken.
.

Place chicken in a baking dish. Bake uncovered at 350° for 45 minutes or until chicken is done.

Chardonnay, Bandol and Beaujolais

Flipped Chicken and Rice
(Riz-bi-dfeen)

Serves 4-6

Ingredients

4 pounds boneless, skinless, chicken
   breasts, cut in small cubes
1 cup uncooked long-grain white rice, washed and drained
4 medium onions, chopped
2 cloves garlic, chopped
1 (15 ounce) can chickpeas, drained
4 tablespoons butter
2 cups chicken broth

Method

In a medium pot, melt butter and sauté onions and garlic until
tender. Add chicken and cook thoroughly.

In another medium pot, combine chickpeas and chicken broth.
Bring to a boil, then add rice, garlic, onions, and chicken.
Reduce heat to low, cook for 30-45 minutes until all the liquid
is absorbed and rice is tender. Let stand for 15 minutes.

Put a platter on top of saucepan, then flip the ingredients onto
the platter. You should see layered chickpeas, rice and chicken.

Nahima's Garlic Chicken and Vegetable Medley

Serves 6

Ingredients

6 boneless, skinless chicken breasts
1 cup green cabbage, cut in large chunks
1 cup cauliflower, cut in large chunks
1 cup broccoli, cut in large chunks
1 cup carrots, cut in large chunks
1 medium onion, cut in large chunks
1 (14.5 ounce) can diced tomatoes, undrained
8 small red potatoes, cut in half
3 cloves garlic, minced
Salt and pepper, to taste
1/2 cup extra virgin olive oil
1 tablespoon lemon juice

Method

In a bowl, combine olive oil, lemon juice, garlic, salt, and pepper. Toss chicken breasts in mixture, then place chicken in a roasting pan. Broil both sides of chicken until brown.

Place vegetables and tomatoes on top of chicken. Cover and bake in 350° oven for 45 minutes or until chicken and vegetables are done.

Garlic Lovers' Chicken
with White Wine

Serves 4

Ingredients

4 boneless, skinless chicken breasts
1/2 cup dry white wine
1/4 cup lemon juice
1/4 cup extra virgin olive oil
20 cloves garlic, whole
1 teaspoon dried thyme
1 teaspoon dried rosemary
1 teaspoon sage
1/2 teaspoon salt
1/4 cup fresh, flat-leaf parsley, chopped

Method

Place chicken breasts in an ungreased baking dish. In a bowl, combine remaining ingredients except garlic. Pour over chicken. Add garlic cloves on top of chicken.

Bake uncovered at 350° for 1 hour. Before serving, sprinkle with fresh parsley.

Sauvignon Blanc

Greek Chicken
with Feta Cheese and Olives

Serves 4

Ingredients

4 boneless, skinless chicken breasts
1 (14.5 ounce) can diced tomatoes, undrained
1/2 cup Kalamata olives, pitted, and cut in half
1 teaspoon dried oregano
2 tablespoons feta cheese, crumbled
2 tablespoons extra virgin olive oil
1 teaspoon lemon juice
Salt and pepper, to taste

Method

In a large skillet, heat olive oil over medium-high heat. Salt and pepper chicken on both sides. Brown chicken for about 5 minutes, turning once.

Stir in tomatoes, lemon juice, olives and oregano. Bring to boil. Reduce heat, cover and simmer on low for 20 minutes until chicken is done.

Remove chicken and place on serving platter. Sprinkle with feta cheese.

Lebanese Chicken
with Allspice and Cinnamon

Serves 4

Ingredients

4 boneless, skinless chicken breasts
1/2 teaspoon ground cinnamon
1/2 teaspoon allspice
2 tablespoons extra virgin olive oil
1/4 teaspoon salt

Method

In a small bowl, combine all spices. Mix well. Pat spices on both sides of chicken.

In a skillet, heat oil over medium heat. Add chicken and cook on both sides until juices run clear.

Gewurztraminer

Lemony Chicken
with Couscous and Pistachios

Serves 4

Ingredients

2 1/2 pounds boneless, skinless, chicken tenders
1 onion, chopped
1 clove garlic, chopped
1/2 cup chicken broth
2 lemons, quartered
1 cup couscous
1/2 cup pistachios
3 tablespoons extra virgin olive oil, divided
1/4 cup fresh mint, chopped
1/4 cup fresh, flat-leaf parsley, chopped
Salt and pepper, to taste

Method

In a large skillet, heat 2 tablespoons of olive oil over medium heat. Add chicken and cook, turning occasionally, until golden brown. Remove and set aside.

In the same skillet, add onion and garlic. Cook over medium heat until tender. Add cooked chicken, broth, lemons, salt and pepper. Simmer, covered on low heat for 15 minutes. Add herbs and pistachios.

In a saucepan, bring 2 cups of water to a boil. Stir in 1 tablespoon olive oil. Add couscous. Stir well. Remove from heat and cover. Let stand 3 minutes. Place couscous on a large platter and top with chicken mixture.

Lemon Chicken
with Pine Nuts and Garlic

Serves 6

Ingredients

4 boneless, skinless chicken breasts
1 tablespoon lemon juice
3 cloves garlic, chopped
1/2 teaspoon ground black pepper
1/2 teaspoon salt
1/4 cup pine nuts
4 tablespoons extra virgin olive oil

Method

Salt and pepper chicken on both sides. Heat olive oil in a large skillet over medium heat. Add garlic, lemon juice and pine nuts. Sauté until light brown. Add chicken and cook on both sides until juices run clear.

Marinated Chicken Kabobs

Serves 12

Ingredients

3 pounds boneless, skinless chicken breasts, cut in cubes
2 cloves garlic, pressed
2 large green or red bell pepper, cut in chunks
1/2 pound fresh mushroom caps
12 pearl onions
12 cherry tomatoes
1/3 cup vinegar (red or white)
4 tablespoons extra virgin olive oil
2 teaspoons salt
1 teaspoon ground black pepper

Method

In a bowl, combine oil, vinegar, garlic, salt and pepper. Add chicken breasts; mix well. Cover with plastic wrap and refrigerate for 3 hours, stirring occasionally.

If using wooden skewers, soak them in water for 10 minutes. Alternate chicken and vegetables. Cook on grill for 30 minutes or until chicken is cooked through, basting with marinade occasionally.

Can also use cubed squash or zucchini, unpeeled.

Nahima's Moist and Tender Fried Chicken

Serves 6

Ingredients

3 pounds cut up chicken
1/2 cup all-purpose flour
1 1/2 teaspoon salt
1/2 teaspoon ground black pepper
Canola oil
Paper bag

Method

Wash chicken and drain until dry or dry with paper towels. Place flour, salt and pepper in a paper bag. Add chicken and shake well until chicken is coated.

In a large skillet heat enough oil to cover bottom. When oil is hot, add chicken and fry on both sides until golden brown. Remove chicken from skillet and lay on paper towels to drain. Place cooked chicken in a vegetable steamer with about 1 inch of water at the bottom. Bring water to boil, reduce heat, cover and steam chicken until moist and tender.

> *Sparkling Wine*
> *(preferably Cava or Prosecco)*

Oven Baked Chicken
with Zattar

Serves 4-6

Ingredients

1 whole roasting chicken
1/2 cup zattar seasoning
1 cup extra virgin olive oil
1 tablespoon salt

Method

Wash chicken, cleaning cavity well, and pat dry. Rub olive oil all over the outside of chicken. Pour or brush oil inside the cavity. Sprinkle inside and out with salt and zattar seasoning.

Place chicken in roasting pan and cover with foil. Bake at 325° for 20 minutes per pound until done. Remove foil during last half hour of cooking to brown top.

Perfect Roasted Chicken
with Pine Nuts and Garlic

Serves 4-6

Ingredients

1 roasting chicken
1/2 cup pine nuts
1 medium onion, cut in fourths
1 tablespoon salted butter
1 tablespoon extra virgin olive oil
1/2 teaspoon allspice (optional)
4 garlic cloves, cut in half
Salt and pepper, to taste

Method

Wash chicken, cleaning cavity well, and pat dry.

In a pan, sauté pine nuts, garlic, allspice, salt and pepper in butter and oil until pine nuts are light brown.

Stuff mixture inside cavity of chicken. Add onions to hold the mixture inside.

Place chicken breast-side up on a rack in a shallow roasting pan. Bake at 325° for 1 to 1/1/2 hours or until meat thermometer reads 180° and juice is no longer pink when center of thigh is cut.

Savory Yogurt Chicken
with Herbs

Serves 4

Ingredients

4 boneless, skinless chicken breasts,
1 cup plain Greek yogurt (store bought)
1/4 cup extra virgin olive oil
2 tablespoons lemon juice
2 cloves garlic, minced
1 tablespoon dried rosemary*
1 tablespoon dried thyme*
1 tablespoon ground black pepper
1 teaspoon salt
Fresh herbs or fresh, flat-leaf parsley for garnish (optional)

*Can substitute 2 tablespoons zattar seasoning for the rosemary and thyme

Method

Combine all ingredients in a bowl or zip-lock bag. Add chicken and marinate in refrigerator for 2 or more hours.

Grill chicken on medium high heat or bake in a 350° oven for 45 minutes until cooked through. Garnish with fresh herbs or parsley.

Nahima's Wings and Green Beans

Serves 6-8

Ingredients

2 pounds chicken wings
1 large onion, chopped
3 cloves garlic, chopped
1 (28 ounce) can diced tomatoes, undrained
1 1/2 pounds fresh green beans
3 tablespoons salted butter
Salt and pepper, to taste

Method

Rinse chicken wings, pat dry and cut off and discard tips. Wash, trim and snap green beans.

In a large pot, melt butter. Sauté onions and garlic until tender. Add chicken wings, salt, pepper and tomatoes. Cover and cook on medium heat until chicken is tender and cooked through.

In another medium pot, cook green beans in enough water to cover. Cook until tender, then place on top of cooked wings. Toss and serve warm.

Desserts & Breads

Arabic Date Cookies

Yield 2 dozen

Ingredients

1 3/4 cup all-purpose or whole wheat flour
1/4 teaspoon salt
1/4 teaspoon ground cloves
3/4 teaspoon ground cinnamon
1 cup nuts of your choice, chopped
1 cup dates, chopped
1 cup sugar
1/2 cup salted butter
2 eggs
3/4 teaspoon baking soda

Method

In a bowl, dissolve baking soda in 3 tablespoons of hot water. Cream butter and sugar. Add eggs and beat until well blended. Add flour, salt, cloves and cinnamon, alternating soda and water.

When well blended, add nuts and dates. Drop by rounded teaspoon on an ungreased cookie sheet and bake at 375° until brown.

> Sweet Sherry (preferably Pedro Ximenez)
> or Tawny Port

Aunt Lee's Nut-filled Cookies
(Ma'amoul)

Yield 3 dozen

Ingredients

2 cups all-purpose flour
1 cup cream of wheat (farina)
1/2 cup salted butter, softened
1/2 cup powdered sugar
1/2 cup pecans, chopped
3/4 cup sugar
1 tablespoon rose water

Method

In a bowl, combine pecans, sugar and rose water; set aside.

In another bowl, combine flour and cream of wheat. Add butter and mix with a fork. Add 2 tablespoons cold water to flour mixture until it is easy to work with. Form into 36 balls. With index finger, make an indentation in the middle of each ball. Fill indention with a teaspoon of nut mixture. Carefully pinch dough, sealing the filling. Flatten with a fork or use a decorative mold to flatten.

Place an inch apart on an ungreased cookie sheet. Bake at 350° for 15-20 minutes or until light brown. Remove from oven and immediately dust with powdered sugar.

Delightful Apricot Bars

Yield 36 bars

Ingredients

1 1/4 cups all-purpose or whole wheat flour
3/4 cup brown sugar
6 tablespoons salted butter, softened
3/4 cup apricot preserves
4 tablespoons dried apricots, chopped

Method

In a bowl, combine flour, brown sugar and butter until well blended. Firmly pat half of the mixture into a 9-inch square pan.

In another bowl, mix together preserves and dried apricots. Spread on top of flour mixture. Top with remaining flour mixture, patting lightly.

Bake for 30 minutes at 350° or until golden brown. Cool 10 minutes before cutting.

Sauternes or Riesling (preferably Auslese)

Oasis Date Bars

Yield 18 bars

Ingredients

3 eggs
1/2 cup light brown sugar
1 cup whole wheat flour
1 teaspoon baking powder
1/8 teaspoon salt
1 teaspoon ground cinnamon
1/2 teaspoon ground cloves
1/2 teaspoon allspice
1/8 teaspoon ground nutmeg
1 teaspoon vanilla
1 cup dates, chopped
1/2 cup walnuts, chopped

Method

In a small bowl, beat eggs until well blended. Gradually add brown sugar.

In another bowl, sift together flour, baking powder, salt and spices. Add eggs and vanilla to flour mixture and beat until well blended. Add dates and nuts.

Spray a 9 x 13 baking pan with non-stick cooking spray. Pour mixture into pan. Bake at 325° for 25 minutes. Cool and cut into bars.

Snow Ball Cookies

Yield 2 dozen

Ingredients

1/2 cup salted butter, softened
1/4 cup granulated sugar
2 cups self-rising flour
2 egg yolks, beaten
1 teaspoon vanilla extract
1 cup walnuts, finely chopped
1/4 cup water
Powdered sugar to roll the cookies

Method

In a medium bowl, combine all ingredients except powdered sugar. Mix well. Form into 1 inch balls. Place on an ungreased cookie sheet. Bake at 350° for 12 minutes. Do not let them get brown. Let cool then roll in powdered sugar.

Syrian Donuts
(Kocke)

Yields 60-80 donuts

Ingredients

6 cups all-purpose flour
6 teaspoons baking powder
1 1/2 cups sugar
1 1/2 cups canola or vegetable oil
1/2 teaspoon salt
3 eggs
2 tablespoons yonsoon
1 cup water
2 cups sesame seeds

Method

In a large bowl, mix all ingredients except eggs and sesame seeds together, adding more water if necessary. Roll into sticks; turn ends together to meet.

In another bowl, whisk eggs and pour onto a flat plate. Place sesame seeds in another plate. Dip top of donut, barely touching, in egg, then dip in sesame seeds. Place on an ungreased cookie sheet. Bake at 300° for 30 minutes until brown.

Hello Della Squares

Ingredients

6 tablespoons unsalted butter, melted
1 cup flaked coconut
1 cup dark chocolate chips
1 cup graham cracker crumbs
1 cup chopped walnuts, or nuts of choice
1 (14 ounce) can condensed milk

Method

In a medium bowl, combine butter, coconut, chocolate chips, graham cracker crumbs, and nuts. Place into a lightly greased 9 x 13 baking dish and pat down evenly. Pour condensed milk over the top. Bake at 350° for 30 minutes until firm. Cool and cut into squares.

Decadent Chocolate Covered Dried Fruit

Ingredients

1 (12 ounce) package semi-sweet or milk chocolate chips
Dried apricots, peaches, or any dried fruit

Method

Line a cookie sheet with waxed paper.

Melt chocolate in a glass bowl in the microwave, stirring frequently until melted.

Dip half of each piece of fruit into the chocolate. Place on waxed paper.

Place in refrigerator until chocolate is hard. Store in airtight container, using waxed paper to separate layers.

Muscat (orange)
(preferably from California)

Nahima's Traditional Baklava

Yield 3 dozen

Ingredients

1 pound package frozen pastry sheets (filo dough), thawed
1 1/2 cups walnuts or pecans, finely chopped
1/2 to 1 cup sugar
1 cup Basic Light Syrup (see recipe page 174)
1 tablespoon rose water
2 pounds Clarified Butter (see recipe page 175)
1 tablespoon salted butter

Method

Butter bottom of a large rectangular pan with a 2" lip. In a bowl, combine nuts, sugar, rose water and 1 tablespoon of tap water. Mix well.

Divide dough in half. Keep covered with a damp cloth to prevent dough from drying. Layer the sheets one at a time, applying clarified butter with a pastry brush to each sheet. After half of the sheets have been layered, place nut mixture on top. Add remaining sheets buttering and layering one at a time.

Cut into squares or triangles. Bake at 300° for 1 hour or until golden brown. Do not overbake. Take out of oven and pour cooled syrup evenly on top.

To store: Layer squares between sheets of waxed paper. Can store in airtight container. Can freeze up to 3 months. Thaw at room temperature.

Basic Light Syrup *(for Baklava)*
(Sharab)

Yield 1 cup

Ingredients

1 1/2 cups sugar
1 cup water
1 tablespoon lemon juice
1 tablespoon rose water

Method

In a medium saucepan, bring sugar and water to a boil over medium heat. Boil until thick. Add lemon juice and continue cooking 5 more minutes. Stir in rose water; cook another 5 minutes.

Pour over any baklava pastry.

Variations:
Add 2 teaspoons grated lemon peel, 2 teaspoons grated orange peel, or 1 teaspoon cinnamon.

Clarified Butter *for Baklava*
(Samneh)

Ingredients

3 pounds unsalted butter (6 cups)

Method

In a medium saucepan, melt butter on low heat until foam appears on top and turns a light brown. Strain through a white clean cloth while liquid is still hot. Keep in the refrigerator until needed. Lasts for several months.

Contemporary Easy Baklava

Yield 2 dozen

Ingredients

8 sheets frozen pastry sheets (filo dough)
3 cups walnuts or pecans, finely chopped
1 cup honey
Rind of 1 lemon, grated
1/2 teaspoon ground cinnamon
Melted butter for cookie sheet

Method

Thaw pastry sheets for 10 minutes and then unroll each sheet. Keep covered with a damp cloth to avoid drying out.

Place 4 pastry sheets on a buttered cookie sheet. Spread 1 1/2 cups of nuts on top in an even layer.

In a bowl, mix honey, lemon rind and cinnamon. Drizzle 1/2 of the honey mixture over the nuts. Repeat layering, ending with 4 sheets of pastry. Keep remaining honey for the end..

Bake at 400° for 25-30 minutes or until puffed and golden brown. Do not overbake. Take out of oven and drizzle with remaining honey. Store in airtight container.

Cool and cut into serving size pieces.

Baklava Fingers

Yield 3 dozen

Ingredients

1/2 pound frozen pastry sheets (filo dough), thawed
3 cups walnuts, pistachios or pecans, finely chopped
1 1/2 cups sugar
2 tablespoons lemon juice
1 teaspoon ground cinnamon
1 cup honey or Basic Light Syrup (see recipe page 174)
1 teaspoon rose water
3/4 cup unsalted butter or Clarified Butter (see recipe page 175)

Method

Separate pastry sheets. Keep dough covered with a damp cloth while using to prevent dough from drying. Brush well with butter.

In a medium bowl, combine nuts, sugar, cinnamon, lemon juice and rose water. Place 3 tablespoons of nut mixture across one end of the dough. Roll up and place on an unbuttered cookie sheet. Brush with butter and cut sticks to desired lengths.

Bake at 350° for 20 minutes or until golden brown. Do not overbake. Let cool and pour honey or light syrup on top.

Remove sticks from cookie sheet with a slotted spoon to drain off excess syrup. Store in an airtight container.

Pretty Baklava Pinwheels

Yield 30 pieces

Ingredients

10 frozen pastry sheets (filo dough), thawed
2 cups walnuts, pecans or pistachios, finely chopped
1 teaspoon ground cinnamon
1/4 teaspoon ground nutmeg
1/3 cup sugar
1/4 teaspoon salt
1 cup Basic Light Syrup (see recipe page 174)
1 pound Clarified Butter (see recipe page 175)

Method

In a medium bowl, combine nuts, cinnamon, nutmeg, sugar and salt. Mix well. Keep dough covered with a damp cloth while using to prevent dough from drying.

Lay one sheet of dough onto a flat surface and sprinkle with nut mixture. Continue this procedure until you have used 5 sheets of dough and half the mixture. Roll pastry like a jelly roll until tight. Slice in 1 inch thick rounds. Repeat process with remaining dough and nuts.

Place pastry rounds on a baking sheet. Drizzle about one tablespoon butter on each circle.

Bake at 350° for 20 to 25 minutes or until golden brown. Pour cooled syrup evenly on top and allow to stand for 1 hour before serving. Store in airtight container.

Sassy Baklava Sticks

Yield 7 dozen

Ingredients

1 pound package frozen pastry sheets (filo dough), thawed
1 pound walnuts, pistachios or pecans, chopped
1/2 cup sugar
1 1/2 cups Basic Light Syrup (see recipe page 174)
3 cups Clarified Butter (see recipe page 175)
1 tablespoon rose water

Method

Combine nuts, sugar, and rose water. Keep dough covered with a damp cloth while using to prevent dough from drying.
Brush a cookie sheet with some of the melted butter. Generously brush pastry sheets, four at a time, with melted butter. Place a teaspoon of nut mixture at one end of the dough, fold ends over about 1" and roll. Place rolls on the cookie sheet. Cut each roll into finger-sized sticks. Dot with remaining butter. Repeat process.

Bake at 350° for 20 minutes or until golden brown.

Drain off extra butter; remove sticks and pour cold syrup over warm sticks. Store in airtight container.

Andrea's Simple Baklava Cups

Yield 30 pieces

Ingredients

2 packages (15 in each) Athenian mini filo shells
1/3 cup honey
2 teaspoons lemon juice
1/2 teaspoon rose water
1 cup walnuts, pistachios or pecans, chopped
3 tablespoons sugar
1/2 teaspoon ground cinnamon
1 tablespoon salted butter, melted

Method

Heat oven to 350°. Place filo shells on an ungreased cookie sheet.

In a small bowl, mix honey, lemon juice and rose water. Blend well and set aside.

In a food processor, chop nuts; add sugar and cinnamon. Add melted butter and pulse to blend well.

Place a rounded teaspoonful of nut mixture into each shell. Bake 8-10 minutes or until light brown. Remove from oven. While hot, spoon about 1 teaspoon of honey mixture over the top. Cool before serving. Store in airtight container.

Turkish Apricot Filo Cups

Yield 15 pieces

Ingredients

1 package (15 each) Athenian mini filo shells
1/2 cup dried apricots, chopped
1/2 cup walnuts
3 tablespoons honey
1/2 teaspoon rose water (optional)

Method

Combine apricots and walnuts in a food processor. Add honey and rose water and blend well.

Place mixture in filo cups on an ungreased cookie sheet. Bake at 350° for 8-10 minutes or until light brown. Remove from oven. Cool before serving. Store in airtight container.

Helen's Rice Pudding
(Rooz Ib Haleeb)

Serves 6

Ingredients

1/2 cup medium-grain white rice, washed, drained
1/2 cup water
3 1/2 cups milk
1/2 cup sugar

Method

In a large saucepan, bring water and milk to a boil. Add rice and sugar. Bring to a boil. Reduce heat to low, uncovered, approximately 45 minutes, stirring often, until rice is soft and creamy.

Remove from heat and let cool slightly, then pour into a bowl and refrigerate. Serve chilled.

Traditional Basic Dough
(Talami)

Ingredients

1 package dry yeast
1/2 cup water
3 cups all-purpose or wheat flour
1 teaspoon sugar
1 teaspoon salt
1/3 cup vegetable oil
1 cup lukewarm water

Method

In a small bowl, soak yeast and sugar in 1/3 cup of water.

In another large bowl, mix together salt and flour. Gradually add oil and work into the flour with your hands. Add lukewarm water and yeast mixture to the flour mixture. Knead until dough is smooth.

Cover dough with plastic wrap and a towel. Let rest and rise at room temperature until dough doubles in size. When dough has doubled, remove enough to make 7" rounds. Roll with hands and place on a lightly greased baking sheet.

Bake at 425° for 10 minutes or until light brown.

Nahima's Syrian Bread
(Aros)

Ingredients

5 pounds all-purpose flour
1 pound salted butter
3 packages active dry yeast
1 quart whole milk
Scant one tablespoon salt
3 tablespoons sugar
1 tablespoon mahleb
1 tablespoon ground fennel seed (shomra)
Bread stamp (munush)

Method

In a large bowl, place flour, reserving a little to coat your hands. Add mahleb, ground fennel seed, salt and 2 tablespoons sugar.

Add yeast to 1/2 cup of warm water and stir. Stir in one tablespoon sugar. Let rise. Add to flour mixture and mix together with your hands.

In a large saucepan, melt the butter on low. Add milk until warm (do not boil). Pour heated milk and butter into the flour mixture.

Knead dough for 15 minutes. Cover with waxed paper and a white cloth and then cover with blankets. Let rise for 2 1/2 hours. Make about 19 round, smooth balls. Let rise until you see the balls expand.

Roll out each ball flat and stamp it with a bread stamp (munush). Also prick with a fork three times for ventilation. Place two flat rounds together, stamped side facing each other, until all rounds are together. Keep them covered with a light white cloth until ready to bake. Let stand under cloth for 20 minutes until puffy.

Bake on an ungreased cookie sheet on bottom rack at 475° for 5 minutes. Move to the top rack until light golden brown. Cool on a cooling rack.

Lebanese Bread Rounds

Yield 15 pieces

Ingredients

5 pounds all-purpose flour
1 cup vegetable oil
2 packages dry yeast
2 tablespoons salt
1 tablespoon sugar
1 cup warm water
3 1/2 cups water

Method

In a small bowl, dissolve yeast in 1 cup of warm water and sugar. Cover and let rise.

In a large bowl, mix flour and salt. Add yeast mixture. Gradually add oil and water, mixing and kneading until dough is smooth. Cover and let rise and rest for 1 1/2 hours.

Form into 15 balls and continue to let them rest and rise with waxed paper on bottom and top. Cover with a blanket. Let rise for another 1 1/2 hours.

Roll into 7-inch rounds. Let rest and rise again for another hour. Place rounds on an ungreased baking sheet. Bake at 425° for 10 minutes or until light brown.

Quick Zattar Bread

Serves 8-10

Ingredients

1 long loaf French bread (baguette), white or whole wheat
Olive oil, to taste
Zattar seasoning, to taste

Method

Cut French bread in half lengthwise. Drizzle olive oil on top and sprinkle with zattar seasoning. Place on an ungreased cookie sheet and bake at 350° until brown and crispy.

Variation:

Use refrigerated biscuit dough in place of French bread. Flatten rounds and drizzle olive oil on top and sprinkle with zattar seasoning. Bake according to package directions.

Sugar and Spice Pita Chips

Serves 4

Ingredients

2 pita bread rounds, split
2 teaspoons sugar
1/4 teaspoon ground cinnamon
Non-stick cooking spray

Method

In a small bowl, combine cinnamon and sugar and mix well.

Cut pita rounds into triangles. Place on a baking sheet. Spray pita with non-stick cooking spray. Sprinkle with cinnamon/sugar mixture.

Bake at 350° for 10 minutes or until light brown.

Can be stored in an airtight container.

Slow Cooker

Chicken and Onion Stew

Serves 6

Ingredients

2 pounds boneless, skinless chicken breasts
2 teaspoons salt
1/2 teaspoon ground black pepper
1/4 teaspoon ground cinnamon
1/2 cup salted butter, melted
2 (14 ounce) cans chicken broth
1/2 cup lemon juice
5 medium onions, sliced

Method

Spray inside of slow cooker with non-stick cooking spray.

Mix salt, pepper and cinnamon and season chicken on both sides. Place in slow cooker. Add onions, broth, butter and lemon juice. Cook on low 8-10 hours or on high 3-4 hours.

Chicken Artichoke
with White Wine

Serves 4

Ingredients

4 boneless, skinless chicken breasts
3/4 cup white wine
3/4 cup chicken broth
1 (14 ounce) can artichoke hearts, drained
3 tablespoons salted butter, melted
2 cloves garlic, minced
1/4 teaspoon dried rosemary
Salt and pepper, to taste

Method

Spray inside of slow cooker with non-stick cooking spray.

Season chicken on both sides with salt and pepper. Place in slow cooker.

In a medium bowl, combine wine, broth, butter, rosemary and garlic. Mix well. Pour over chicken. Add artichokes on top. Cover and cook on low 8-10 hours or on high 3-4 hours.

Silvaner or Gruner Veltliner

Chicken Tarragon and Tomatoes

Serves 4

Ingredients

4 boneless, skinless chicken breasts
8 medium mushrooms, sliced
3 tablespoons onions, finely chopped
1 cup dry white wine
1 (14.5 ounce) can diced peeled tomatoes, undrained
1/4 teaspoon dried thyme
1 cup long-grain white rice, uncooked
2 tablespoons melted butter

Method

Spray inside of slow cooker with non-stick cooking spray.

Place chicken in bottom of a slow cooker. Combine remaining ingredients and place on top of chicken. Cook on low 8-10 hours or on high 3-4 hours.

White Burgundy or
White Bordeaux

Fragrant Chicken
with Cauliflower and Rice

Serves 4-6

Ingredients

6 boneless, skinless chicken breasts, cut in small cubes
1/4 cup long-grain white rice, uncooked
2 1/2 cups chicken broth
1 (16 ounce) bag frozen cauliflower, thawed
2 tablespoons curry powder
Salt and pepper, to taste

Method

Spray inside of slow cooker with non-stick cooking spray.

Place rice in the bottom of a slow cooker and sprinkle with salt and pepper. Top with the chicken cubes. Pour remaining ingredients over chicken. Cover and cook on low 8-10 hours or on high 3-4 hours.

Easy Chickpeas and Chicken

Serves 4-6

Ingredients

2 pounds boneless, skinless chicken breasts
1 (14 ounce) can chicken broth
1 large onion, cubed
2 cloves garlic, sliced
1 (15 ounce) can chickpeas, drained

Method

Spray inside of slow cooker with non-stick cooking spray.

Place onions and garlic in slow cooker. Add chicken and broth. Cover and cook on low 8-10 hours or on high 3-4 hours. Add chickpeas during last hour of cooking.

Classic Greek Chicken
with Vegetables and Olives

Serves 4

Ingredients

4 boneless, skinless chicken breasts
3 large white potatoes, unpeeled, cut lengthwise in eighths
3 large carrots, cut in thirds
2 medium onions, quartered
3 cloves garlic, cut in half
1/2 cup whole kalamata olives, pitted
2 tablespoons lemon juice
1/4 cup white wine
1/2 tablespoon dried oregano
1/2 teaspoon salt
1/2 teaspoon ground black pepper

Method

Spray inside of slow cooker with non-stick cooking spray.

Place vegetables in slow cooker. Add chicken breasts and remaining ingredients.

Cover and cook on low 8-10 hours or on high 3-4 hours.

Lebanese Flipped Chicken and Rice
(Riz-bi-dfeen)

Serves 4

Ingredients

4 boneless, skinless chicken breasts, cut in small cubes
2 large onions, chopped
1 clove garlic, minced
1/2 teaspoon ground cinnamon
1/2 teaspoon ground black pepper
1/2 teaspoon allspice
1 teaspoon salt
2 (14 ounce) cans chickpeas, drained
1 cup long-grain white rice, uncooked
1/2 cup salted butter, melted
2 (15 ounce) cans chicken broth

Method

Spray inside of slow cooker with non-stick cooking spray.

Place chickpeas, onions, garlic and spices in bottom of slow cooker. Add rice, chicken and broth. Cover and cook on low for 8-10 hours or on high 3-4 hours.

To serve, place a serving platter on top of slow cooker and flip contents onto platter.

Whole Chicken Mediterranean
with Zattar

Serves 6

Ingredients

1 roasting chicken
3 medium onions, chopped
3 tablespoons zattar seasoning
3 garlic cloves, whole
1 tablespoon salt
2 teaspoons ground black pepper
2 tablespoons salted butter, melted
1 teaspoon dried parsley
1 teaspoon dried basil
1 teaspoon dried rosemary
1 teaspoon dried thyme
3 tablespoons extra virgin olive oil
1 (14 ounce) can chicken broth

Method

Spray inside of slow cooker with non-stick cooking spray.

Place onions and garlic in bottom of slow cooker.

Put melted butter in cavity of chicken. Mix herbs together and add to cavity. Salt and pepper outside of chicken. Rub olive oil on top and rub zattar seasoning all over chicken. Place in slow cooker.

Cover and cook on low 8-10 hours or on high 3-4 hours.

Chickpea and Ham Soup

Serves 4-6

Ingredients

1 pound ham, cubed
2 (15 ounce) cans chickpeas, drained
4 cloves garlic, cut in quarters
1 cup celery, chopped
1 cup carrots, diced
2 medium onions, chopped
2 teaspoons dried parsley
4 cups chicken broth
Liquid smoke, to taste
Salt and pepper, to taste

Method

Spray inside of slow cooker with non-stick cooking spray.

Place all ingredients in a slow cooker. Cover and cook on low 8-10 hours or on high 3-4 hours.

Pinot Noir
(preferably Oregon)

Pork Chops and Green Beans

Serves 4

Ingredients

4 boneless pork chops
1 medium onion, chopped
3 garlic cloves, chopped
1 (15 ounce) can diced tomatoes, undrained
1 (12 ounce) package frozen green beans
Salt, pepper and garlic powder, to taste

Method

Spray inside of slow cooker with non-stick cooking spray.

Place onions and garlic in slow cooker. Sprinkle salt, pepper and garlic powder on both sides of pork. Lay pork on top of onions. Add tomatoes.

Cover and cook on low 8-10 hours or on high 3-4 hours. Add green beans during last hour of cooking.

Succulent Pork Tenderloin
with Kalamata Olives

Serves 4-6

Ingredients

1 pound pork tenderloin
1/2 cup kalamata olives, whole, pitted
1/2 cup chicken broth
2 tablespoons lemon juice
2 tablespoons extra virgin olive oil
2 cloves garlic, chopped
Oregano, dried
Salt and pepper, to taste

Method

Spray inside of slow cooker with non-stick cooking spray.

Rub olive oil, oregano, salt and pepper over tenderloin. Place in slow cooker. Add garlic, olives, lemon juice and chicken broth. Cover and cook on low 8-10 hours or on high 3-4 hours.

Dry Rose', Riesling or Rioja

Beef and Lima Bean Stew

Serves 4-6

Ingredients

2 pounds sirloin, cut in cubes
2 large onions, chopped
2 teaspoons salt
1 teaspoon ground black pepper
2 (10 ounce) packages frozen lima beans
1 (10 ounce) can tomato sauce
2 cups water
2 cloves garlic, chopped

Method

Spray inside of slow cooker with non-stick cooking spray.

Place ingredients in slow cooker in order given. Cover and cook on low 8-10 hours or on high 3-4 hours.

Chickpea, Beef and Vegetable Stew

Serves 6

Ingredients

2 pounds round steak, cut into 1 inch cubes
2 (8 ounce) cans tomato sauce
1 tablespoon Worcestershire sauce
1 teaspoon paprika
2 (14 ounce) cans beef broth
2 celery stalks, cut in 1/2" slices
3 carrots, peeled and cut in 1/2" rounds
1 tablespoon dried parsley
1 (15 ounce) can chickpeas, drained
8 red potatoes, unpeeled, cut in half
2 cloves garlic, cut in half
2 bay leaves
1 (10 ounce) package frozen peas
1 large onion, chopped

Method

Spray inside of slow cooker with non-stick cooking spray.

Place steak in bottom of slow cooker. Add remaining ingredients. Cover and cook on low 8-10 hours or on high 3-4 hours. Remove bay leaves before serving.

Mediterranean Beef Kabobs
with Vegetables

Serves 8-10

Ingredients

3 pounds sirloin tip beef
2 large green bell peppers, cut into cubes
1/2 pound fresh mushroom caps
12 cherry tomatoes
1 large onions, chopped
2 cloves garlic, cut in half
1/2 cup lemon juice
1/4 cup Worcestershire sauce
1 cup extra virgin olive oil
3/4 cup soy sauce
1/4 cup prepared yellow mustard
Ground black pepper, to taste

Method

Spray inside of slow cooker with non-stick cooking spray.

Trim fat from beef and cut into 1 1/2 inch cubes.

Combine lemon juice, Worcestershire sauce, olive oil, soy sauce, and mustard in a bowl. Mix well.

Place meat in slow cooker. Add vegetables, onion and garlic. Pour lemon juice mixture over top. Cover and cook on low 8-10 hours or on high 3-4 hours.

String Beans and Meat

(Yuknee Lubee)

Serves 4

Ingredients

1 pound cubed sirloin or meat of choice
1 pound fresh string beans or 1 (16 ounce) package frozen beans
1 (14 ounce) can diced tomatoes, undrained
1 medium onion, diced
2 cloves garlic, chopped
3 tablespoons extra virgin olive oil
1 (8 ounce) can tomato sauce
Salt and pepper, to taste

Method

Spray inside of slow cooker with non-stick cooking spray.

Place green beans, onion, and garlic in slow cooker. Salt and pepper the meat. Place on top of beans. Add tomatoes and sauce. Cover and cook on low 8-10 hours or on high 3-4 hours.

Simply Succulent Shrimp Soup

Serves 6

Ingredients

1 pound medium raw shrimp, peeled and deveined
2 (14 ounce) cans chicken broth
1 (8 ounce) can tomato sauce
4 green onions, chopped
1/2 medium green bell pepper, chopped
1/2 medium red bell pepper, chopped
2 cloves garlic, minced
1/2 cup fresh mushrooms, sliced
1/2 cup kalamata olives, pitted and sliced
1 teaspoon dried oregano
1 teaspoon dried basil
1/8 teaspoon ground black pepper
1 (6 ounce) container sour cream

Method

Spray inside of slow cooker with non-stick cooking spray.

Combine all ingredients except shrimp and sour cream in a slow cooker. Cover and cook on low 8-10 hours or on high 3-4 hours, adding shrimp during last hour before serving.

Add a spoonful of sour cream on top of each serving.

Mediterranean Shrimp Soup

Serves 6

Ingredients

1 pound pre-cooked, peeled shrimp, tails removed
1 medium onion, chopped
1/2 of a medium green bell pepper, chopped
2 celery stalks, chopped
2 cloves garlic, minced
1/4 cup kalamata olives, pitted and sliced
1 (14.5 ounce) can diced tomatoes, undrained
2 (14 ounce) cans chicken broth
1 (8 ounce) can tomato sauce
1 tablespoon dried parsley
1 teaspoon dried basil
1 teaspoon dried thyme
1/2 cup dry white wine

Method

Spray inside of slow cooker with non-stick cooking spray.

Combine all ingredients except shrimp in a slow cooker. Cover and cook on low 8-10 hours or on high 3-4 hours, adding shrimp during last hour before serving.

Mediterranean Vegetable and Lentil Soup

Serves 6

Ingredients

1/2 cup dried lentils, rinsed and drained
4 cloves garlic, chopped
1 large onion, chopped
1 1/2 teaspoons ground coriander
1 1/2 teaspoon ground cumin
1/2 teaspoon ground cinnamon
1/2 teaspoon ground black pepper
1/2 cup celery, chopped
1 medium yellow squash, chopped
1 medium zucchini, chopped
1 (14.5 ounce) can diced tomatoes, undrained
1/2 cup green bell pepper, chopped
1/2 cup fresh, flat-leaf parsley or 2 tablespoons dried parsley
1 teaspoon dried basil
3 3/4 cups chicken broth

Method

Spray inside of slow cooker with non-stick cooking spray.

Combine all ingredients in a slow cooker. Cover and cook on low 8-10 hours or on high 3-4 hours.

Sensational Eggplant
(Moussaka)

Serves 4

Ingredients

1 pound ground chuck
2 medium eggplants
2 small onions, chopped
3 cloves garlic, minced
1 (8 ounce) can tomato sauce
1/2 cup red wine
2 tablespoons salted butter, melted
1/4 teaspoon ground cinnamon
1/4 teaspoon ground nutmeg
2 tablespoons dried parsley
1/2 teaspoon dried thyme
1/2 teaspoon dried rosemary
1/2 cup Parmesan cheese, grated
4 tablespoons extra virgin olive oil
Salt and pepper, to taste

Method

Spray inside of slow cooker with non-stick cooking spray.

Peel and dice eggplant. In a large saucepan, sauté eggplant in butter until golden brown. Remove from pan and set aside. Add olive oil and sauté onions and garlic until tender. Add beef and continue cooking until beef is brown. Add herbs, salt and pepper. Stir well. Place eggplant, meat mixture, tomato sauce and wine in a slow cooker. Cover and cook on low 8-10 hours or on high 3-4 hours. Top with cheese before serving.

Arabian Chili
with Chickpeas

Serves 4-6

Ingredients

1 pound ground beef or ground turkey
2 (15 ounce) cans chickpeas, drained
2 (15 ounce) cans diced tomatoes, undrained
1 (1.25 ounce) package chili seasoning
1 (6 ounce) can tomato paste
2 cloves garlic, chopped

Method

Spray inside of slow cooker with non-stick cooking spray.

In a skillet, brown meat over medium heat until done. Drain and transfer to a slow cooker. Add remaining ingredients. Cover and cook on low 8-10 hours or on high 3-4 hours.

Zinfandel

Nahima's Special Spaghetti
with Worcestershire Sauce

Serves 6-8

Ingredients

2 pounds chicken wings
1 large onion, chopped
1 (14.5 ounce) can diced tomatoes, undrained
1 (8 ounce) can tomato sauce
1 (5 ounce) Worcestershire sauce
1 (16 ounce) package spaghetti
Fresh basil or fresh, flat-leaf parsley for garnish

Method

Spray inside of slow cooker with non-stick cooking spray.

Rinse wings, pat dry and cut off and discard tips. Place in slow cooker.

Place remaining ingredients except spaghetti in a bowl and mix well. Pour over chicken. Cook on low 8-10 hours or on high 3-4 hours.

Cook spaghetti al dente according to package directions. Drain and place in a casserole dish. Pour chicken and sauce mixture on top and mix well. Garnish with fresh basil or parsley.

> Barbera
> (preferably New-World or ripe Italian)

Chicken and Eggplant
with Pine Nuts

Serves 4

Ingredients

4 boneless, skinless chicken breasts
1 medium eggplant, peeled and cut into 1" cubes
1 large tomato, peeled, seeded and coarsely chopped
3 cloves garlic, minced
1 bay leaf
2 tablespoons pine nuts
1/3 cup extra virgin olive oil
1/2 teaspoon sugar
1/3 cup chopped fresh, flat-leaf parsley
Pinch of cayenne pepper
Salt, to taste

Method

In a saucepan, sauté eggplant in olive oil over medium-low heat for 2 minutes until oil is absorbed.

Spray inside of slow cooker with non-stick cooking spray.

Place chicken in bottom of slow cooker. Combine remaining ingredients and place on top of chicken. Cook on low 8-10 hours or on high 3-4 hours. Remove bay leaf. Before serving, sprinkle with parsley.

Notes

Notes

Notes

Notes

Notes

Notes